making home your happy place

making home your happy place

A Real-Life Guide to Decluttering Without the Overwhelm

KATY WELLS

W Publishing Group

An Imprint of Thomas Nelson

Making Home Your Happy Place

Published by W Publishing, an imprint of Thomas Nelson, 501 Nelson Place, Nashville, TN 37214, USA.

The author is represented by Alive Literary Agency, www.aliveliterary.com.

Thomas Nelson titles may be purchased in bulk for educational, business, fundraising, or sales promotional use. For information, please email SpecialMarkets@ThomasNelson.com.

ISBN 978-1-4003-4823-7 (audiobook)
ISBN 978-1-4003-4822-0 (ePub)
ISBN 978-1-4003-4821-3 (TP)

HarperCollins Publishers, Macken House, 39/40 Mayor Street Upper, Dublin 1, D01 C9W8, Ireland (https://www.harpercollins.com)

Library of Congress Control Number: 2025945473

Art direction: Meg Schmidt
Cover Design: Connie Gabbert
Interior Design: Kristina Juodenas

Printed in the United States of America

25 26 27 28 29 LBC 5 4 3 2 1

To Andrew, River, and Levi:

Thank you for filling my days with laughter, love, and so much grace. For the ordinary moments that feel extraordinary simply because we share them. Doing life with you is my greatest joy.

To my parents, sister, and brother—thank you for your unwavering love and the roots that shaped me.

And to every woman who's ever whispered, "I want a simpler life, but I don't know where to start"—this is for you. May these pages remind you that you're not alone. You're more capable than you know.

Contents

Chapter 1

Less Managing, More Living

Some moments divide your life into *before* and *after.* This was one of those moments. At 9:05 a.m. on November 24, 2017, everything changed.

The screech of tires. The deafening crunch of metal. Then—silence.

Time had slowed as the force of the head-on collision slammed me forward against my seat belt. Smoke poured into the car, thick and suffocating. My ears buzzed, my heart pounded, and my brain raced to make sense of the chaos: We'd been in a car accident.

I blinked, and reality slowly came back into focus. Andrew, my husband, was motionless, slumped over the steering wheel, the front of the car crumpled around him. Fear gripped me as I twisted to check the back seat. My boys—just one and two years old—were crying but unharmed. Thank God.

The smoke thickened, each breath burning as panic clawed its way through my chest. I yanked at the door handle. Nothing. My hands shook as I pounded on the window, screaming for help, my voice raw and desperate.

Ten minutes earlier, Andrew and I had loaded up the van, buzzing with excitement. We'd been heading to the National Gingerbread House Competition in Asheville, North Carolina, prioritizing family fun after another exhausting week of work, home tasks, and parenting. "This will be so fun," I'd told Andrew. "We need this."

Yes, there still were piles of dishes, loads of laundry, and cluttered counters to take care of—but I'd get to that later. Taking in Andrew's smile and the kids' little legs happily wiggling in their car seats, I'd felt a rare moment of calm and relief from a constant, gnawing feeling that I wasn't enough. For the first time in days, I'd let out a deep, satisfying breath—the kind of breath that comes when you finally step out of survival mode, even briefly.

I couldn't have imagined that only ten minutes later, firefighters would be shattering our van's back windshield and carefully maneuvering my sons to safety using calm but urgent voices. Or that my husband would stir and murmur, "I can't feel my hands," before slipping back into unconsciousness.

Next, a firefighter guided me out of the van through the jagged opening in the back. My boots crunched over broken glass, the sharp sound cutting through the haze. I sank on to the curb, clutching my babies tightly as their small bodies trembled against mine. My mind and body were in complete shock, caught in the surreal blur of those moments.

I'll never forget the sound of the saw they used to cut out Andrew's car door. The metallic whine of the Jaws of

Life—something I'd only ever seen in movies—was now carving its way through my Honda Odyssey.

At the hospital, the medical team rushed Andrew into the intensive care unit, while I got an X-ray to check for a broken elbow. My racing thoughts kept circling back to the same haunting questions: *Will he survive? Will he walk again? What would I do without him?* The emotional weight of the unknown—and the frightening possibilities—was unbearable. Somewhere in the swirl of white coats and fluorescent lights, I realized that our life had just split in two: the one we used to have, and the one we were about to face.

As the day went on, I tried to stay strong for everyone who kept checking in, nodding at what the doctors said, responding to every text message, not allowing myself to show emotion. But inside, I was overcome by a strange numbness. In the span of just a few hours, I'd gone from thinking about dinner plans to wondering if my husband would ever walk again. The shift was sudden and unforgiving.

Several hours passed in a fog of waiting rooms, whispered prayers, and frantic phone calls to family. Finally, a doctor came to report, "He's stable, but it's going to be a long road to recovery. He has multiple neck fractures, a broken shoulder, and a punctured lung."

Despite the list of injuries, I felt relief wash over me. He was still with us, and I was endlessly grateful. Then a crushing wave of exhaustion quickly followed. The adrenaline that had left me numb enough to manage through the day was gone, leaving me hollow.

By the time 9:00 p.m. rolled around—twelve hours after the accident—it was time for me to go home.

Our boys had spent the day at my friend's house while her parents watched them, and now she and another close friend were driving me home with the boys in the back seat. As we pulled into the driveway, I exhaled, hoping that stepping into the familiarity of home would give my mind a place to rest. But the moment I opened the door, chaos greeted me like an unwelcome guest.

Toys were scattered across the floor—magnetic blocks, DUPLO blocks, and tiny action figures. Half-broken crayons and scraps of coloring books covered the couch. Dirty dishes were piled high in the sink, and unopened mail and art supplies cluttered the kitchen counters.

It was like the chaos of the accident had followed me home, spilling into every corner of my house. The clutter mirrored how I felt inside—overwhelmed, out of control, and suffocating. My gaze darted from mess to mess, each one pulling me deeper into a spiral of shame and anger.

How did I let it get like this? I needed peace, a moment to breathe, but instead, my home felt like a battlefield.

My friends didn't say a word as they started picking up toys and washing dishes. I stood there, paralyzed, fighting back tears.

This wasn't how it was supposed to be. This wasn't the life I wanted.

The weight of it all—the clutter, the mess, the constant feeling of failure—pressed down on me. I felt exposed and painfully aware of how out of control my home had become.

Feeling Buried in the Overload

That night, when I finally crawled into bed, I was too exhausted to sleep. My body was still, but my mind wasn't. It kept racing through everything I'd seen, felt, and carried that day. Amid the swirl of emotion, one thought repeated on a loop: *I can't keep living like this.*

It wasn't the first time I'd had that thought. It had been tugging at me for a while—one of those thoughts that doesn't scream but simmers under the surface, begging for change.

I'd tried everything (maybe you have too): marathon decluttering weekends that left me more drained than free. Color-coded bins that were supposed to make life easier but added more things to manage. Even Marie Kondo's joy-sparking technique, which, for a moment, gave me hope. But nothing ever stuck. I'd spend hours organizing one space, only to have the clutter resurface somewhere else. It was like playing an endless game of Whac-A-Mole, and I was losing.

Lying there in the dark, I replayed the events of the day in my mind—the accident, the ambulance ride, the hospital, the X-rays, the ICU, the ride home—and how, after all of it, I'd stepped into a house that felt like chaos. I was punched in the gut by the mess, the overwhelm, the shame, the sheer weight of trying to hold it all together.

That's when something unexpected clicked.

I realized the clutter hadn't just been distracting me; in a strange way, it had been shielding me. If I stayed busy shuffling the same stack of mail, reorganizing the kids' toys for the hundredth time, or digging through an overflowing junk drawer, I didn't have to acknowledge what else was going on in my life. I didn't have to face the feelings I didn't want to feel. I didn't have to confront the dreams I had quietly abandoned or the parts of myself I didn't even recognize anymore. Clutter wasn't just filling my home. It was filling the gaps in my life—the longings, the losses, and the needs I didn't know how to name.

Andrew's recovery was long and grueling. He spent months in a neck brace, undergoing physical therapy and navigating the slow, painful process of healing. But in time, he did heal—and for that, I'm still deeply grateful.

Still, the experience shook something loose in me. I had hoped home would be the place where we could begin to recover—a space to hold us through the hardest season of our lives. But as I stood in the middle of that cluttered living room, it was painfully clear: Our home wasn't supporting us. It wasn't offering peace or comfort. It was demanding more from me when I had nothing left to give.

We often hear that clutter steals our time, our presence, and our joy. It does, but it also can serve as a cover. It can buffer us from the uncomfortable truths, buried emotions, and parts of ourselves we've tucked away for later, when the chaos of life lifts.

As we move through life, obligations gradually start to accumulate. Like a painting left untouched for years, hidden beneath layers of dust, *we* can get buried over time too. At first, we hardly notice. A little mess here. A busy season there. We convince ourselves we'll catch up—when work slows down, when the schedule lets up, when life isn't *so much*.

But as the years go on, the layers keep building, and somewhere along the way, the vibrant, alive version of us may get dulled. Maybe we forget what used to make us laugh, spark ideas, or bring rest. We might wake up one day surrounded by clutter—physical, mental, emotional—and hardly recognize the person staring back at us in the mirror.

If you're thinking, *That sounds like me,* I want you to know: You're not the only one, and you don't have to go on feeling this way. What's buried can be uncovered. What is underneath has always been there—the version of you who feels lighter and freer, who knows how to rest and be present in her home. She isn't lost. She's just been covered up.

This is the power decluttering holds; it isn't just about getting rid of stuff. It's about getting honest—gently, over time—about who you are, how you're doing, and what you really want from your life. Not in a pressure-filled way. Not with a five-year plan. With just enough honesty to take the next step. Little by little, you restore what's always been there and make space for who you are becoming.

Now, it could be your story feels different. Maybe things aren't falling apart, but they're not really coming together either. You're not drowning, but you're treading water. You're managing the home, the schedules, the expectations—but it still feels harder than it should. You've decluttered before, maybe even read the books and bought the bins, but your systems haven't stuck. If that's you, you belong here too.

Whether you're at rock-bottom or just want something simpler, steadier, and more sustainable, this book will give you a way forward. Even more, it'll open up new possibilities of where to put your energy. If a lot of it is currently going into managing your stuff, there can't be much left for nurturing your peace, your passions, your people—or yourself.

When you uncover what matters most and clear the clutter, you don't just create space; you reclaim your life.

Finding the Right Way to Dig Out

Now, does this mean it's time to go on a frantic, throw-everything-out purge? Or invest in another set of perfectly labeled bins?

Nope. You don't need more pressure or some unrealistic system. You need a new perspective—one that gives you permission to take steady steps toward what matters. You need a strategy that's individual to you, based on the deeper realities driving your habits.

You heard me right: Decluttering isn't just about clearing surfaces. It's about discovering *what's causing the clutter,* because that's the only way real, lasting change happens.

For years, I missed that. I approached decluttering like a checklist: Clear off the countertops, sort through the kids' clothes, tidy the entryway (again). While those things helped in the moment, the clutter always came back—even when I was following all the expert advice.

I didn't realize I was treating symptoms, not healing the cause.

I was donating, labeling, and tidying, but I was still stuck in the same cycles because I hadn't addressed what was causing the clutter. The beliefs. The habits. The emotional weight.

Finally I got to the point when I stopped asking "How do I fix the mess?" and started asking "What's keeping me stuck?"

That's when I started creating the Holistic Decluttering Method. I thought, *If a holistic approach to health looks at the whole person, not just their symptoms, what if we did the same with our homes?*

It would mean not just focusing on the stuff but the emotions and stories tied to it. Not just cleaning up the space but shifting the habits and systems that shape it. Not just learning *how* to declutter but uncovering the deeper *why*.

As I followed that path, everything changed.

In this book, I want to show you how it can change for you too.

Holistic Decluttering

By now, you might be wondering, *Okay, but how much is she going to ask me to get rid of? Is this one of those "you can only own two pairs of jeans and four forks" kind of book? Do I have to toss half my closet and every backup spatula to keep up?*

No.

We've all been sold the idea that less stuff equals less stress, but Holistic Decluttering isn't about minimalism checklists. Why chase someone else's version of simplicity when you can develop your own? Why chase momentary perfection instead of creating lasting peace in a way that works for you?

Most decluttering methods treat the surface. They chop off the visible weeds so things look better for a little while. But if the root is still there—if the soil hasn't changed—the clutter always grows back.

Holistic Decluttering doesn't just chop the weeds; it pulls them out at the root. Then it helps you plant something new. Peace. Clarity. Confidence. A home that feels the way you want it to.

Using this method starts by focusing on three key areas:

- **Root awareness:** We identify the beliefs, emotions, and habits that keep us stuck, like guilt, fear of waste, or "What if I need it?" thinking. And we learn how to move forward without shame.
- **Empowered action:** We take intentional, doable steps that free up space—not only in our home, but in our mind and heart.
- **Sustainable momentum:** We build habits and systems that stick, so our progress doesn't fizzle out after one weekend sprint.

Before this kind of Holistic Decluttering, I was a *no* mom.

No, we can't play—I need to clean up this mess. No, I can't read one more bedtime story—the laundry's beeping at me again. No, I can't sit down—I still have a million things to catch up on.

The clutter (physical, mental, and emotional) was always calling for my attention. I'd waste so much time simply looking for things. I was constantly spinning in circles trying to keep up with managing our stuff. Even the simplest joys felt out of reach.

But as I began clearing space, not only in my home but in my heart, something shifted. I became a *yes* mom.

Yes to baking cookies, because the counters were clear. Yes to one more story, because I wasn't running on empty. Yes to impromptu dance parties in the living room, because the weight of "unfinished chores" was no longer pulling me away.

Holistic Decluttering didn't just make my house easier to manage. It helped me show up differently inside of it. Day by day, clarity brought freedom. My home felt lighter—and so did I. I could welcome friends in without a frantic cleanup. I could sit and play Uno with my boys, fully present—not side-eyeing a pile in the corner or mentally rearranging my to-do list.

In clearing the clutter, I didn't just find space; I found myself again. And in finding myself, I reconnected with the values I wanted to build my life around.

The more I let go, the more decisions seemed easier. I became more intentional with my time. And for the first time in a long time, I felt like I wasn't simply reacting to life—I was fully living it.

Now, years later, that still holds true. The clarity, the lightness, the presence—it wasn't a phase. It has become my new normal.

I know it can become yours too.

And I'm here to walk with you as you discover that.

How to Use This Book

This book is your companion, a resource to encourage, inspire, and guide you as you create a home that feels lighter and supports you. Each chapter is packed with mindset shifts and doable steps designed to help you make progress, build momentum, and create lasting change—without the overwhelm.

What I'm sharing in this book isn't simply theory; it's the fruit of years of trial, error, prayer, and transformation. These strategies have helped thousands of women and families create calm in the middle of chaos, and they continue to shape my own home and life today.

In the pages ahead, I'll show you how to let go of the physical clutter as well as the emotional weight that's been silently shaping your days. If you're tempted to jump to the part of the book that feels most urgent for you, I get it. But I want to encourage you to start at the beginning and move through each chapter one step at a time. Trust me, it's worth it. Each chapter builds on the last, working in tandem to help you create the peace you've been craving.

You'll learn how to:

- **Uncover the deeper roots of clutter.** Discover the emotional ties, habits, and beliefs that keep you holding on and how to let go with clarity and compassion.
- **Start making progress with confidence.** Learn how to take that first step—even if you're feeling

overwhelmed—and build momentum that fits into your life.

- **Transform your space and mindset.** Move beyond surface-level fixes to reclaim your time, energy, and mental clarity for the things that matter most.
- **Build systems that support you.** Create simple routines and rhythms that help you maintain your progress without constant effort.

This is more than tidying. It's transformation, and it happens through small steps you can start taking every day. Each chapter is designed to meet you where you are—no shame, no pressure—so you can take the next right step toward a home (and life!) that feels lighter, calmer, and full of possibility.

Chapter 2

Your Stuff Story

Imagine sitting in a theater, playbill in hand, anticipation buzzing. The show's about to begin. But the curtain never rises and the lights stay dim—even as the performance begins.

You can hear the actors' muffled dialogue and footsteps across the stage. You catch pieces of emotion: a laugh here, an outburst there. You lean forward, straining to understand. Why is he stomping? Why is she crying? Without the visuals, you're lost.

Believe it or not, this type of frustration and confusion is what you can experience in a cluttered space. It happens when you live in a home shaped by a Stuff Story you haven't uncovered yet.

What's a Stuff Story? It's the invisible script that shapes how you relate to your belongings. It was written over time by the people who raised you, the culture you grew up in, and the messages you picked up about safety, success, shame, and what a "good" home should look like. It's not something you chose. It's something you inherited.

Most of us are living in stories we never meant to write.

When you stand in your home, you're surrounded

by objects that hold meaning, memories, and messages that you absorbed long before you ever lived there. Maybe you were taught that letting go of things is wasteful—that you should hang on to things even when they no longer serve you, just in case. Maybe you grew up in a home where scarcity was real, and having backups brought comfort. Maybe your mom cleaned late into the night, and now clutter doesn't just feel messy; it feels like irresponsibility. A silent accusation that you should be doing more.

These stories don't announce themselves, yet they shape every decision. They're the reason why, after a weekend purge, clutter creeps back in and you find yourself wondering, *Why is this still so hard? Is there something wrong with me?*

Let me tell you what I wish someone had told me sooner: There's nothing wrong with you. You're not lazy, and you're not bad at this. You're reacting to a story that hasn't been fully told yet—so you might feel like you would in a theater with no visuals.

Here's the kicker: Your brain has built habits around that story, compensating for what it can't visualize. You're operating with default neural patterns, which were always meant to keep you safe and help you be efficient—but now, they're keeping you stuck.

In this chapter, we're going to pull back the curtain and finally see the full stage. You need to be able to see not only the clutter in front of you but the stories behind it. The beliefs that shaped you. The emotional weight that's been hitching a ride on your possessions for years.

You'll start to recognize the script and learn how to rewrite it—so you can live out a new story that is rooted in compassion, conviction, and freedom.

How Your Brain's Default Patterns Keep You Stuck

Have you ever walked into a room intending to declutter, then find yourself standing still? You know what needs to go, but something inside resists. What's that hesitation about?

It's wiring.

Your brain is designed with one job above all else: survival. To your nervous system, survival means sticking with what's safe, familiar, and predictable. Even if what's familiar is clutter.

Over time, your brain starts building patterns, shortcuts that help you cope with discomfort, uncertainty, or emotional weight. If that pile in the corner has helped you feel "on top of things," or if those junk drawers have distracted you from grief or burnout—your brain has been doing its job.

Maybe you've used clutter like a buffer, something to busy yourself with when the deeper feelings seem too big to face. Maybe clutter has given you a false sense of readiness for the what-ifs ahead. Maybe holding on to things helps you avoid making the tough decisions laced with guilt, nostalgia, or fear. Whatever your version looks like, those patterns were meant to protect you, not sabotage you.

The problem is, these protective patterns don't usually shut off when you outgrow them. Instead, they become your brain's default operating system. So even when part of you craves clarity and calm, another part clings to the comfort of the old way. Not because you're lazy—but because you're loyal to what's felt safe.

Psychologists call this *cognitive fluency*. It's your brain's preference for what's easy, predictable, and familiar. Dr. Bruce Lipton, a leading voice in neuropsychology, explains that about 95 percent of our behavior is driven by subconscious programs, meaning we operate on autopilot most of the time while the conscious mind directs only about 5 percent of our actions.[1] Unless we pause and consciously rewrite the script, we'll keep repeating the same scenes. It's like your brain is still running old software designed for a past season, not the story you're living now.

The first step toward change is awareness, because you can't rewire what you can't see. It's like pulling back the curtains in that dark theater; suddenly, you can recognize what's been running the show.

The best way to begin is by tracing your patterns back to their origins—to the powerful forces that formed you:

- **Your upbringing and home environment:** whatever was modeled for you about keeping, spending, saving, and "being prepared"
- **Your personal experiences:** the moments that tied emotions (such as grief, scarcity, shame, or pride) to your stuff

- **Cultural conditioning:** the messages (spoken and unspoken) that told you more stuff equals more success, love, safety, or status

Together, these formed the silent blueprint for how you relate to "stuff." This is your Stuff Story. Once you see it, you can finally stop wondering, *Why is this so hard?* and start moving forward with understanding.

Historical: The Patterns You Inherited

The way your parents or caregivers managed their possessions—what they chose to buy, repair, keep, or toss—often becomes the silent script for how you manage your own.

Think back to your childhood. Was your home filled with "just-in-case" items, or did your family regularly declutter? Was your mom committed to a spotless home, always scrubbing and straightening, even if it meant missing moments of connection? Or was she comfortable with a little mess in exchange for time together?

These early experiences don't just fade; they imprint. They shape what we subconsciously believe a "good" home should look like and how we should care for it.

Maybe you've caught yourself mirroring those patterns. If your parents saved everything, you might struggle to let go, thinking, *What if I need this later?* If they were constantly decluttering, you might feel pressure to keep your home minimal, or swing the other way and hold on to everything as an act of rebellion.

These beliefs often have deep generational roots. My grandfather, for example, grew up during the Great Depression—a time when frugality wasn't just a value but a means of survival. Letting go of anything, even broken or useless items, felt reckless, so he didn't.

Those habits informed his definition of *normal*, which trickled down to his children—including my mom—and, eventually, to me.

Survival led to habits, and habits became inheritance.

But here's the powerful part: You don't have to embrace what you inherited or pass it down to someone else. You're allowed to pause and question what was handed to you, asking *Does this still serve me?* You're allowed to sift through the stories and choose which ones you want to carry forward.

This isn't about looking for someone to blame. It's about understanding your history and being intentional about where you go from here.

Personal: Your Own Experiences

No matter what your upbringing was like, every item in your home holds some kind of meaning or message, even if you've never stopped to consider it before.

Some meanings are obvious: A family heirloom that reminds you of someone you love. A photo album filled with childhood memories. A baby blanket you swore you'd pass down someday.

Other meanings are more subtle. They live in the corners of closets and the back of drawers, layered with hope, identity, and maybe a little regret. They're associated with the versions of ourselves we've been, the ones we're trying to become, and the stories we're not sure we're ready to close.

You're allowed to sift through the stories and choose which ones you want to carry forward.

You don't keep the blazer from your old job because it's "nice." You keep it because it reminds you of a time when you felt sharp. Needed. Certain.

You don't keep the treadmill because you love cardio. You keep it because part of you still believes that using it might turn you into the woman you thought you'd be by now.

Maybe it's dishes for dinner parties that never happen. Books for quiet weekends that never come. Craft supplies for the creative version of you who's been waiting for time that never shows up on the calendar.

These aren't just things. They're placeholders for dreams you're still attached to. For identities you're not sure you're ready to let go of.

And when those items accumulate, they take up not only room in your home but also emotional real estate. They whisper stories in the background, shaping how you see yourself and what you believe is possible.

But here's the truth: Letting go doesn't mean giving up on who you were or who you'll become. It means making space for who you are now.

Cultural: The Claim That More Is Better

Now for the final component of your Stuff Story: the cultural forces that have shaped what you believe about success, safety, and what a "good life" should look like.

From the time we were kids, we've been surrounded by messages telling us that happiness is just one purchase away. Cartoons came with jingles, cereal boxes came with toys, and suddenly our joy felt tied to whatever we didn't have yet. As adults, those messages just got savvier. Sleek ads. Influencers. Pinterest-perfect homes.

Now the promise is, *Buy this, and you'll be happier. More confident. More beautiful. More successful.*

And for a moment, it works. You get the thing. Feel a little spark. A small lift. Then the high fades, and you chase the next one.

Then it becomes a loop: This time it'll stick. This time I'll feel different. But it never does. Because it was never really about the stuff.

It was about identity.

A luxury car doesn't just get you places. It says something about who you are. A designer purse? Not just fabric and stitching. It's a badge, a signal. Even toothpaste isn't just toothpaste—it comes with the promise of a brighter smile and new charm.

We're not simply buying products. We're buying feelings, stories, belonging, and the hope that this next purchase will finally make us feel the way we've been longing to feel.

We live in a culture of consumption—and "too much." Too much noise. Too much pressure. Too much more. It's a toxic undercurrent of modern life. We're taught that full equals good. If your calendar isn't packed and your home isn't full, it must mean you're falling behind. So we rush to fill every inch—of our homes, our calendars, our lives.

And the flip side of that message? Emptiness feels like lack. A blank space on your calendar seems wasteful. A bare countertop seems unfinished. A quiet afternoon feels wrong.

Space means something is missing, we are told.

But what if it doesn't? What if space is where peace begins? What if less isn't insufficiency but freedom?

What if the solution isn't adding but unlearning?

You don't have to keep playing the game no one ever wins—proving your worth through what you own, do, or achieve.

You get to choose a different story.

Take a minute to picture yourself back in that theater, but you're no longer sitting in the dark, trying to piece together the plot. The curtain has lifted, the lights are on. You're no longer catching scattered bits of dialogue—now, you're seeing the full scene with its characters and context. And in that clarity, you finally understand: Oh . . . This is what I've been reacting to all along.

You then come to realize: This play is about *you*. Your life, your habits, and how those decisions have affected your home. And in fact, you are not only the audience, but rather, the writer. The one calling the shots on what happens next.

This is what it's like to recognize the forces that shaped your Stuff Story and see what's been driving your relationship with stuff. With the lights on, you can name it, explore it, and question it. You get to decide which parts still fit and which parts you're ready to rewrite.

Challenging the Old Programming

For years, my client Brooke felt trapped in a cycle she couldn't break. She could see the clutter—the extra linens no one used, the toys her kids had long outgrown, the clothes collecting dust in her closet. She *knew* what she needed to do. But every time she tried to let go, her body tightened. Her hands would hover over an item, then freeze.

It wasn't that she didn't want a simpler home. It was that something inside her seemed to say, *You can't let that go.*

Brooke had grown up in a house where they saved everything. "You never know when you might need that" was less of a suggestion and more of a family motto. Her parents had inherited that mindset from their parents—and eventually, those words became hers too.

What once served her family as a survival skill had become her own stuck point. Every decision to declutter triggered not just a task but a tangle of guilt, fear, and uncertainty.

And with every stalled attempt, a new belief took root: I'm not an organized person.

It became her mantra. Not because it was true but because it explained the stuckness, and it gave her a reason to stop trying. Brooke didn't lack motivation. She had tried the Pinterest printables, the "just one drawer" advice, the viral tidying methods. But none of them worked because none of them addressed the real issue: the internal programming that told her she wasn't allowed to let go. No checklist could override that deeply ingrained messaging that said, *Hold on to it—just in case. Letting go would be wasteful and careless.*

Until one day, mid-coaching call, something shifted. We weren't talking about stuff anymore. We were talking about safety. Identity. The story she'd been handed and never thought to rewrite.

And Brooke, courageously, decided to challenge that story.

After one of our calls, she walked into a part of her home that had always kept her stuck. The kind of space she usually avoided—too overwhelming, too layered, too loaded. But this time, she stepped into it holding something new: the truth of her Stuff Story.

She wasn't just standing in front of bins and shelves anymore. She was standing in front of beliefs.

She knelt beside a box of baby clothes. Opened a drawer filled with "just-in-case" items. Reached for ones that had always felt impossible to let go of. Then she burst into tears—out of sheer relief. For the first time, she wasn't just trying to declutter. She was understanding how she'd gotten there. And in that understanding, everything softened.

"I finally get why I couldn't do it before," she whispered. "It's not just about the stuff. It never was."

That moment changed everything. She didn't need to declutter her whole house overnight. She simply needed a new script, one she could return to again and again:

- "Letting go doesn't mean I'm being irresponsible."
- "Releasing what I don't use doesn't mean I'm being wasteful—it means I'm honoring what I actually use and love."
- "Uncertainty doesn't have to stop me. I can feel unsure and still take the next step."

And that's what Brooke did. Even when doubt crept in, she chose to challenge the preprogrammed ideas. She knew that she wasn't just organizing things; she was reclaiming her story.

That same invitation is waiting for you.

Permission to Start Letting Go

By now you know that you are not stuck with the story you were handed. You get to update the script, deciding what stays and what shifts. The next step is not to go toss everything you own in a fit of motivation, but to start recognizing the old programming and gently choosing a new response. One that feels aligned with who you are *now*—not who you were *then*.

That's what Brooke did, and here's why it worked: Each time she repeated a new belief, like "Letting go doesn't make me irresponsible," she wasn't only calming her fears. She was laying down new mental tracks, rewiring her brain through repetition.

Neuroscientists call this neuroplasticity—your brain's ability to form new connections.[2] The more often you practice a new belief, the more natural it becomes. It starts to feel less like a stretch and more like your truth. Eventually, that new belief becomes second nature. No longer something you're trying to believe, but something you do.

As you've begun shining a light on your Stuff Story, have you already felt something loosen? Naming the deeper *why* behind your clutter could help you release something that's been holding you back for years. If that feels out of reach right now, that's okay too. There's more ahead. More tools, more support, more chances to peel back the layers and uncover what's really been keeping you stuck. You're just getting started.

You don't have to have it all figured out. You just need a starting point and a bit of permission to take the next right step. And I've got some ideas for you here at the close of this chapter.

You're doing beautifully. And I'm so proud of you for choosing this path.

Let's keep going.

REFLECT

Take some time to consider the historical, personal, and cultural influences shaping your Stuff Story.

- Are you holding on to things because of family messages about frugality or waste?
- Do certain items tie you to a past version of yourself or a future version you feel pressure to become?

- Have cultural narratives made you feel like the next purchase, the next "fix," the next accomplishment will finally make you feel worthy?

I know that looking back can feel overwhelming. Maybe you're thinking, I don't have time for this kind of deep work—or, I'm not sure I want to open that door.

I get it. But here's the good news: You don't need a full-day retreat or a thirty-page journal entry. You just need a thread of awareness. One belief, one memory, one pattern that makes you go, Huh. Maybe that's why I do that. That moment of recognition is enough to begin. Once you can name something, you can start to loosen its grip.

So ask yourself: What's one belief, habit, or expectation from my Stuff Story that I'm ready to challenge—or gently let go of?

TAKE ACTION

Once you've chosen a belief you're ready to let go of, think of a new belief that better supports the life you're creating.

Write it down. Keep it visible. Let it anchor you when you feel stuck in indecision. Say it out loud sometimes when you want to implement it. The more you repeat it, the more it will become your new default. And the more your thoughts shift, the more your space—and your story—will begin to shift too.

Chapter 3

The Good Enough Home

I have this old sweatshirt—soft, oversized, and worn at the cuffs. It's at least a decade old and definitely not stylish. There's a stain on the sleeve I've never been able to get out. But I love it. It's the sweatshirt I reach for when I need comfort or when I want to feel grounded. When I need to remember that I don't have to perform; I just get to *be*. It's not perfect, but it's perfectly mine.

I wonder if that's the kind of home we're all craving. Not one that looks like a magazine page but one that lets us exhale. One that says, *You belong here, exactly as you are.* Somewhere along the way, I stopped reaching for that kind of comfort—both in my clothes and in my home. I started chasing something more refined, something closer to "perfect." It seemed like if I could feel more put together, I'd feel like I was enough.

But instead, I ended up in a humbling moment that led to a turning point.

One typical weekday, I came home from running errands, arms full of grocery bags, and was instantly hit with the weight of the mess. The smell of last night's dinner still lingered in the air. The dishwasher was half loaded, a towel lay balled up in the hallway, and a stack of unopened mail teetered on the counter. Laundry was draped over the couch like a bunch of dropped costumes. Shoes were scattered across the floor like confetti after a party.

My son tugged at my sleeve. "Mommy, will you play with me?"

Without even thinking, I snapped, "Not now!"

I'll never forget the look on his face.

But what hit me hardest was the voice in my head, harshly asking, *Why can't you get it together?*

I set the groceries down and just stood there, frozen in frustration and exhaustion. I was upset because of the mess—but also because the mess seemed to indicate I was failing as an adult. If I were more disciplined, more organized, more like all the "perfect people" out there, this wouldn't be happening.

Later that week, I sat in my therapist's office, ugly crying over mom guilt. The room smelled faintly of lavender. A clock ticked softly in the background, steady and unfazed. My infant was in his car seat beside me, and I rocked it gently with my foot as I spoke.

I hadn't even meant to unload about the house. I'd come in thinking I'd talk about sleep deprivation or the mental load or why I felt so disconnected from my husband. But when she asked how I was doing, it all spilled out. The shame. The frustration. The exhaustion in my bones.

The mess made me feel like I was drowning, I told her. The state of my home seemed to mirror all the ways I was falling short. I couldn't keep up with the laundry, let alone the life I thought I was supposed to be living.

I fully expected her to nod and offer tips—maybe a

time-blocking trick or some productivity advice. That's what I thought I needed: a better plan.

Instead, she listened quietly, then said something I'll never forget: "Have you ever heard of *good enough parenting*?"

I bristled at the phrase. Good enough? It sounded like giving up or settling. In my mind, "good enough" was what you said when you didn't care anymore. It sounded like mediocrity—and mediocrity terrified me.

But then she explained, "Good enough doesn't mean careless. It means consistent. Present. Responsive, not perfect. It's not about never making mistakes. It's about repair. Kids don't need flawless parents. They need connected ones."

It was the first time someone had told me that the goal wasn't perfection but presence, and research backed it up.

British psychoanalyst Donald Winnicott coined the term *good enough mother* in the 1950s, and it's still used today in child psychology. His studies found that when a parent consistently shows up with empathy and responsiveness—not perfection—it actually builds resilience in children.[1]

This revelation was eye-opening for me. If I could embrace being a good enough parent, could I offer that same grace to myself in my home? Could I stop trying to prove my worth with a spotless kitchen? Could I stop evaluating myself as a person based on the state of the laundry room and the piles of clutter?

Could I believe, maybe for the first time, that I was not the problem?

The shame wasn't as loud when I walked through my door that night. Instead, there was silence. Space. The tiniest beginning of grace.

After that moment, another realization took root: *It's not just that I've been holding myself to an impossible standard. It's that the methods I've been taught were designed to serve that standard.*

The strategies I'd been using looked simple on the surface. Perfectly organized, color-coded bins; minimalist closets; a system so streamlined it seemed like it ran itself. But it all hinged on perfection and was built for a version of life that didn't look anything like mine. A version without toddlers melting down in the hallway or a job that stretched into the evening or a body that needed rest instead of another round of laundry at 10:00 p.m. For me, these methods often delivered burnout and frustration when I couldn't keep up.

That's when the idea of a Good Enough Home started forming in me. Not as a backup plan but as an awakening. I wouldn't be settling; I'd be reclaiming my time, my peace, my life.

My new definition of success became having a home that was easy to tidy, not always spotless. I needed something functional and joyful, not magazine-worthy.

The Good Enough Home

A Good Enough Home isn't about unrealistic standards like sushi-rolled socks or spotless floors. It's not curated for social media. It replaces *Be better* with *You're already enough.* A Good Enough Home is a space that works for you and your people and supports your rhythms—that gives back more than it takes. As it prioritizes connection over perfection, it softens around your chaos instead of shaming you for it.

Early on, a Good Enough Home started freeing me to do things I used to think I didn't have bandwidth for. One night I left the dishes in the sink and sat at the kitchen table with my boys, listening to them passionately debate whether chocolate or vanilla ice cream was superior. I didn't step away to wipe the counters or even try to multitask. Instead, I stayed. That moment—that simple, sticky, beautiful moment—was more nourishing than a spotless kitchen ever had been.

Maybe for you, it'd mean feeling free to go for a walk or getting extra rest after dinner.

In a Good Enough Home, we stop apologizing for the dishes in the sink. We don't let the state of the countertops determine whether we're available for a good conversation. We know every tiny effort counts and that sticking with *good enough* will allow us to do more life-giving things.

There's margin here. There's breathing room. There's space to linger, laugh, and live.

If this is starting to sound a little like giving up, let me clarify: This is not the absence of effort. It's the presence of grace. It's letting go of impossible standards so you can create a space that works with your life, not against it. That shift alone—believing that your home can serve you, support you, and meet you where you are—is powerful.

Letting grace in and forgetting perfection also does a deeper work in us: It disarms shame, and shame is what keeps us stuck. As Brené Brown has explained, "Shame corrodes the part of us that believes we can change and do better."[2] Research shows that shame often makes us want to shut down, pull back, or pretend the problem isn't there—keeping us stuck.[3] But replacing shame with grace? That's what gives us access to hope and the energy to take one small step forward.

Mess Versus Clutter

So, if you want to embrace a Good Enough Home, where do you start?

By learning the difference between mess and clutter.

Sometimes we look around our home and everything feels like a problem—the dishes, the laundry, the piles of stuff. It all blends together into one giant, overwhelming weight. But the reality is, not all mess is clutter, and not all clutter is mess.

Mess is expected. Clutter is optional. And neither says anything about your worth.

Mess is the evidence of life happening. It's cyclical, temporary—and, yes, often feels never-ending. Dirty dishes after dinner. Shoes by the door. Laundry that somehow multiplies even after you just emptied the basket. These are signs that people live here. That you live here.

Instead of feeling defeated every time the hamper fills up or the kitchen gets messy again, I've started to expect it.

When I *expect* mess, it doesn't catch me off guard. It doesn't tempt me to spiral into shame. It becomes part of the rhythm of real life.

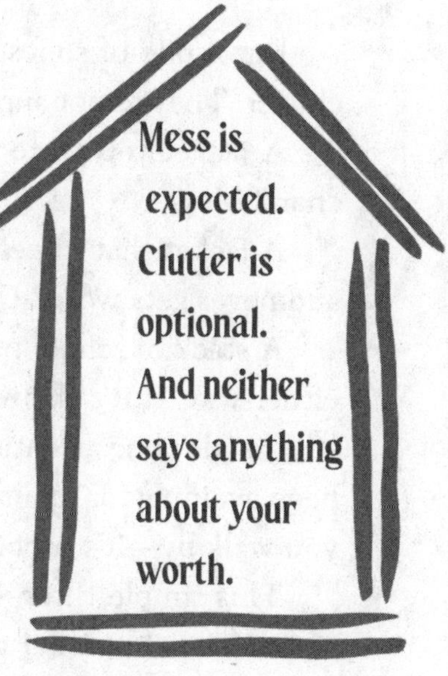

Clutter, on the other hand, is the stuff that no longer serves you, like the broken blender or the jeans that haven't fit in years. It's anything in your home that's no longer actively supporting your life or your values. It could be a box of art supplies for a hobby you never had time to start, or gear from a past life—or an aspirational one—you're not living.

These items aren't bad; they simply aren't serving you in your current season. They also could be taking up emotional bandwidth, draining your energy without giving anything back.

Once I could name the difference between clutter and "expected mess," the weight started to lift. I stopped assigning meaning to messes. I didn't have to assume a pillow fort meant I was behind. I didn't have to resent the laundry for existing.

The mess was still there, but the shame wasn't. I'd shifted from striving for perfection to knowing what actually needed my energy. I could walk through my house and see socks on the stairs or a stack of dishes, then ask myself: *Is this mess or clutter?*

For example, a pile of shoes by the door? That's mess. They're in use; they just need a home or a quick reset.

But a pile of shoes no one's worn in two years? That's clutter. They're not supporting anyone's life right now.

A jacket you wore yesterday tossed over the back of a chair? Mess.

A jacket that's been sitting in the closet for six winters and never gets worn? Clutter.

A stack of school papers on the counter? That could go either way. If it's this week's homework or something that still needs your attention, it's mess. But if it's a pile you've been avoiding for months—and it's adding stress every time you walk by—it's probably clutter.

This simple filter—*Is it mess or clutter?*—will help you respond to the visual noise differently. One needs a reset. The other may need to be let go.

Now let me show you one simple practice that can help you begin managing expected messes—without burnout: the Daily Reset.

Daily Resets: A Piece of the Good Enough Home Puzzle

A reset is a short, intentional tidy-up that restores one specific area of your home back to its baseline—whatever "tidy enough" looks like for you. It's not about scrubbing grout or clearing every drawer, but instead, making a space feel functional, calm, and ready to support you again.

Before she found resets, Kelly felt completely buried in her home office. Piles of papers and half-used notebooks covered her desk. Memorabilia and random cords filled shelves, and boxes with years-old documents were stacked in the corner. Every time she walked in, her shoulders tensed. As it became a source of daily tension, her focus disappeared.

So she avoided it altogether because the clutter felt overwhelming—too big, too far gone.

"I need to declutter this whole room, but I don't even know where to start and I don't have time!" she told me.

I paused, then offered something unexpected. "What if we don't start with decluttering? What if we start with a reset?"

Kelly looked at me, confused. "You want me to tidy up my desk? I'm drowning in clutter, and you want me to start with putting pens away?"

I smiled. "I get it. But this isn't about ignoring the clutter. This is about lowering the temperature. Right now, your brain is in survival mode. Let's give it a win—something small, something doable. Ten minutes. Just clear the top of your desk. Don't dive into the drawers. Don't open the boxes of old photos or keepsakes. Just focus on what's right in front of you. Reset the surface to a calm baseline. That's it."

Kelly was hesitant. But the next day, she gave it a shot.

A few days later, she reported back. "Okay, that actually helped. The rest of the room still needs work, but I feel different just sitting here. Like I have a little more control again. I'm feeling so motivated!"

One reset. One cleared surface. One moment where she reclaimed her space—and her capacity. That ten-minute reset didn't solve everything, but it gave her the confidence to begin. And from there, we gently stepped into deeper clutter work—layer by layer, decision by decision.

This is exactly why I want you to start with resets too. Not because your clutter doesn't matter. But because your brain—and your nervous system—need a safe place to begin.

Resets aren't just a practical tool. They're foundational. They help you build the muscle of noticing what you use, what you love, and what's actually supporting your life. They ease the overwhelm, lower the noise, and help you see your space with new eyes. And maybe most importantly, they remind you that small actions count. You can make progress, even when everything feels like too much.

You can make progress, even when everything feels like too much.

Resets aren't a distraction from decluttering. They're the doorway into it. Because once you start feeling calmer and a little more in control, the deeper work starts to feel possible.

Incorporating Daily Resets

Here's how Daily Resets could look in different areas of your home.

- **The kitchen after dinner:** wiping down the counters, loading the dishwasher, clearing surfaces so you can start the next day fresh.
- **The living room before bedtime:** folding throw blankets, fluffing pillows, putting remotes in their spot and other odds and ends where they belong.

- **The entryway:** hanging up jackets and bags, putting away shoes, clearing dropped mail or packages.
- **Your desk at the end of the workday:** filing stray papers, returning pens to a container, closing your laptop, setting out what you'll need for the next day.

Once you complete a reset, you receive a satisfying signal: This space is back to supporting me. And when that happens? You breathe a little deeper. You feel a little clearheaded. Instead of asking, "Where do I even start?" you already know.

Resets like these can become a daily rhythm for you. With minimal effort from you, they pack a powerful punch.

- **Resets prevent mess from spiraling.** Instead of waiting until your space is completely out of control, resets help you stay ahead of the mess by tackling it in small doses.
- **Resets free your mind to focus.** Knowing a reset is coming gives you permission to *let the mess be* for now. You'll stop trying to micromanage every sock, spoon, or cereal bowl the moment they're out of place.
- **Resets are sustainable.** They don't rely on willpower or a big chunk of time. They meet you where you are (with your busy life, real home, limited energy) and work *with* you.
- **Resets help you spot clutter.** You'll start to notice what's always out of place or never used—and those moments are invitations to let go of what's not serving you. (We'll talk about handling clutter in the next chapter.)

Resets don't need to be big to be effective. They're flexible, forgiving, and can meet you exactly where you are. The full-time employee resets her living room before bed, so mornings feel lighter. The mom of toddlers resets while dinner cooks. The retiree resets after grandkids leave, savoring the moment before restoring the calm. Even three resets a week can shift the tone of your entire home.

If you're thinking, *What if my pets or my roommates undo it within an hour?* Welcome to the club. The reset isn't only about the result; it's about the rhythm. The act of choosing calm, even when chaos is nearby.

Before I got into a reset rhythm, evenings were chaos. The kids would go to bed, the house looked like a tornado, and I'd sit there stewing—too tired to clean, too overwhelmed to rest. Now, the mess still happens, but the guilt doesn't spiral because I know I've got a way back to calm. I've got the Good Enough Home philosophy.

A Reset Isn't Only for Your Home—It's for Your Hope

If the thought of establishing a rhythm sounds daunting, don't worry; you don't have to reset every space every day. You don't have to get anything perfect here! You don't even have to believe in it all the way yet. I only suggest you try it out. Because every time you reset a space, every time you take a small, imperfect step toward calm, you'll be sending yourself a message: *I'm not behind. I'm allowed to breathe here.*

That's what this chapter has been about—redefining your relationship with your home. You can let go of the idea that mess means failure or that only perfectly tidy homes are worthy of peace and pride. Your home doesn't need to be spotless to support your life and bring you joy. You can stop chasing the impossible and start creating something functional and strong. Slowly, little by little, your home will become what it was always meant to be: a place that holds you and serves you. A Good Enough Home. Your happy place.

If you had told me a few years ago that I'd feel calm sitting in a living room with books on the floor and dishes in the sink, I would've laughed. But now I see those things differently—they're signs of life—and my mind can rest knowing I've got a plan for handling it. My regular reset later will create order. Sure, mess can still be annoying, but it doesn't undo me anymore. I know exactly how to meet it and move forward. For me, it started by deciding to have a Good Enough Home and building new rhythms that fit my life.

If you're still thinking, *I don't know if I can do this,* that's okay. You're not behind and you're not too far gone. These are skills you are learning and building that provide a path to the home you want.

Let's keep going.

REFLECT

Look around your space—or picture the one that weighs on you most. What do you see? Is it expected mess? Is it clutter? Is it both?

Maybe even more important: What story are you telling yourself about it?

You don't need a strategy or a label maker. Just notice. That's the first shift.

TAKE ACTION

You can do your first reset like this.

1. **Pick a reset zone.** Focus on a spot where mess piles up quickly (like your kitchen counter or entryway).
2. **Tie the reset to something that's already part of your daily rhythm.** Decide you'll do it after dinner, at the end of the workday, or before bed. Anchor it to your real-life routine.
3. **Keep it simple.** Don't aim for Pinterest. Simply restore it to what feels *good enough* for you.

You don't need to reset your whole house. You just need one clear surface and one choice to say, "This space supports me again."

After you do it one day, try to do it the next too. See if you can bring that reset into your daily rhythm.

Chapter 4

Superficial Clutter

When I was a kid, my dad could turn a stack of lumber into just about anything. One summer, he built us a treehouse. No instructions, no precut pieces; just a rough sketch, a wood pencil behind his ear, and the kind of quiet confidence that comes from doing things by hand. One Saturday, he invited me to help.

I still remember the smell of sawdust in the air, the buzz of cicadas in the trees, and the way his pencil squeaked as he drew a line across the wood. Eager to get started, I grabbed the hammer and said, "Okay, what do we build first?"

He chuckled, the way parents do when they see the whole picture before their kids do. "Eventually we'll build," he said. "But first, we measure."

We didn't touch the hammer for *hours*. There were clamps to set, holes to drill, boards to level. At one point, I remember holding the hammer awkwardly in my hand, unsure of what to do with it—and feeling a little frustrated.

I wanted to be helpful. But I didn't know which tool came next, or why the hammer wasn't the right choice.

Looking back now, I realize what my dad knew all along: You don't build anything with just one tool. Yet that's exactly what most of us try to do when we declutter.

We're handed one method. One rule. One "magic" system. And we're told it should work for everything and everyone.

"Just toss what you haven't used."

"Only keep what sparks joy."

"Get some bins and organize it better."

Sometimes it works. A drawer gets cleared. A cabinet feels lighter. You feel that quick hit of relief. But then the clutter creeps back. What worked in one room completely stalls in another. Before long, you're overwhelmed by stuff all over again.

Why? Because you've only been handed a hammer when what you need is a full tool belt.

The Four Types of Clutter

Have you ever wondered why one room feels easy to clear out while another leaves you feeling completely stuck? It's because not all clutter is the same. Each type holds a different story, a different emotion, and a different reason it's been hard to let go. Every item of clutter is tied to your Stuff Story in a particular way. And just like a builder wouldn't use a hammer for every step of the job, you need a different tool for each type of clutter.

Let's start by looking at the four types of clutter you have in your home.

Superficial Clutter

This is the easiest type to identify and release. It's not tied to memories, guilt, or fear; it has simply overstayed its welcome. It doesn't carry emotion; it has just been overlooked. Life got busy. You didn't have a system. And the clutter quietly stacked up.

You might not even notice it anymore because it's hiding in plain sight:

- half-empty shampoo bottles under the bathroom sink
- supplies you no longer use or want
- duplicate gadgets crammed in drawers
- mismatched plastic containers taking over the kitchen

While superficial clutter is the easiest clutter to deal with, it does still hold weight in your life. It creates background stress and drains your energy, one ignored object at a time.

Scarcity Clutter

Scarcity clutter is rooted in fear: fear of not having enough, of wasting, of letting something go and then needing it later. "Just-in-case" clutter comes from a desire to be prepared, and at one point, it made sense to have each item.

But now these items may be taking up mental space rather than bringing functionality to your life.

You know this kind of clutter when you see it:

- old cords and chargers "just in case"
- clothes you don't wear now but "might someday"
- kitchen gadgets you never reach for but "could be useful"
- a stash of reusable tote bags spilling from the closet

It may be time to let these things go. If you do, you won't be wasteful for releasing what no longer serves you. You'll be reclaiming space for what matters to you now.

Sentimental Clutter

These items hold stories, moments, and milestones. They're about connection, not usefulness—and that's what makes it so hard for you to let go of them. They take you back to a memory that's meaningful:

- a handwritten note from your dad you received as a kid
- a race bib that represents a proud accomplishment
- the wedding dress you'll never wear again
- a shoebox filled with your child's baby shoes

Evaluating sentimental clutter isn't just about clearing a shelf. You're deciding which parts of your story you want to carry forward and which parts you're ready to release with love.

Identity Clutter

This clutter shows up in the gap between who you were, who you thought you'd be, and who you think you should become. It carries quiet pressure, whispering things like, *You used to be creative* or *You should be working out more.* That pressure makes it hard to see what truly supports the life you're living now.

Some of these items reflect a former version of yourself you've outgrown:

- business books from a career that's no longer relevant
- crafting supplies from a hobby you haven't touched in years

Others belong to an aspirational version of yourself:

- books you "should" read, but don't really want to
- a fancy yoga mat you've never unrolled
- cookbooks for a lifestyle you've never had

Letting go of identity clutter isn't about giving up. It's about realigning with who you are and making room for who you're actively becoming.

Now that you know the four types of clutter, we'll spend a chapter discussing the most effective tool and approach for each one. As you move through each chapter, it might be a little like peeling an onion. Not because the four types of clutter are literally connected to each other, but because the difficulty of handling each layer varies. The outer layer comes off easily, with just the lightest touch. As you peel deeper, though, the layers get stickier. More complex. Sometimes, they sting.

Clutter works the same way. The first layer that we'll start with, superficial clutter, is light and loose. You might have already started working on it without realizing it. Addressing it won't require emotional excavation or hours of your time—just a few moments, a little focus, and the right frame of mind.

Most importantly, you'll need the right tools in your hand. Let's get you equipped.

Five Basic Decluttering Steps

First, a quick recap: Superficial clutter is the stuff that piles up because life is full. You didn't intend for your drawer to become a graveyard for promo pens, or your pantry to double as a spice museum. It just happened because you've been busy doing life.

Here are five simple steps designed to help you clear clutter quickly and confidently.

1. Determine an item's "home" and boundary lines.
2. Identify how it actively serves your present life.
3. Ask if you've had the chance to use it.
4. Choose to keep, donate, or sell it.
5. Free up headspace by removing it.

You can use these steps for any type of clutter, but we're

starting with the easiest layer so you can get more fast wins and build momentum.

Each step tackles a specific roadblock. By using all five of them together, you'll be creating a home that reflects your values, supports your daily routines, and feels lighter and more manageable.

Let's take a look at each one.

1. Determine an Item's "Home" and Boundary Lines

Before we talk about what stays and what goes, let's talk about where it's allowed to live. Your home's overall space has limits, so you need to set limits on your stuff too. When you don't, it spreads. Fast.

That's where physical boundaries come in. It can be as simple as using a container to help you define enough and stop the sprawl.

Let's say your kitchen cabinet is overflowing with mugs. Instead of pulling each one out and agonizing over whether you like it enough, try deciding, "I'll keep enough to fit this one shelf." Then work within that boundary, focusing less on whether each mug sparks joy and more on what fits inside the space you've defined.

Boundaries shift the goal from "declutter everything" to "fill this space with only what serves me." It's a clear stopping place, a built-in finish line. And when you can see the end, it's easier to start.

One of my students, Laura, thought she needed some kind of revolutionary hack to deal with the chaotic bathroom drawer she opened every single morning. But once she set a clear boundary for how many products she wanted to see and use, everything shifted. She used small containers to define space for only the essentials. No more digging, no more daily overwhelm. In her words, "Seeing less in that space gives me a calmer start to the day." It wasn't fancy. It was just a boundary—and it worked.

Your "enough" line will look different depending on the space, the season, and your family's needs. When my boys swapped LEGOs for football gear, our toy bins shrank while our sports shelf grew. That was our life flexing—and our boundaries flexing with it.

2. Identify How It Actively Serves Your Present Life

Once you've set your boundaries, the next question is, "What purpose does this item serve in my life right now?" Not someday. Not if things were different. But right now—in the life you're actually living today. This question moves you from the infinite galaxy of *what if* to the grounded reality of *what is*. You're no longer orbiting possibilities and floating in indecision. You're standing on something solid: your real life, your actual needs.

Maybe you've been holding on to a stack of takeout menus. When was the last time you used one? Most places have online menus now, so that pile is more of a habit than a help.

Or maybe there's a spiralizer in your kitchen drawer that was supposed to revolutionize dinnertime. But you've reached for it how many times in the past year? (Be honest.) Is it doing the job it's supposed to do for you?

When you focus on whether something is fulfilling its purpose, you can stop keeping things out of duty and start curating what actually supports you. You're being real, not ruthless. You're not randomly tossing stuff out! You're aligning your home with the version of you who exists today—not the one from five years ago or the one you're "supposed" to be someday. This mindset can make decluttering feel empowering instead of exhausting. Every time you choose what stays for a reason that matters to you, you can know you're creating a home that serves your real life today.

3. Ask If You've Had the Chance to Use It

When you're not sure whether an item is fulfilling its purpose in your present life, you don't need to debate it for twenty minutes. And you need something better than a "maybe" pile. Instead, ask yourself, *Have I had the opportunity to use this in the last six to twelve months?* Notice the shift: it's not *Did I use it?*—it's *Did the opportunity even exist?*

If the answer is yes, but you still haven't used it, that's a clue. Maybe it's buried in the back of a cabinet. Maybe it's too much of a hassle to grab. Or maybe—truthfully—you just like something else better. That tells you something.

If the answer is no, you're probably holding on to it "just in case."

Still unsure? Give that item one last shot by pulling it into your daily space. Move it to the front of a drawer or somewhere else you'll easily see it. Then set a reminder to check back in a month or two. If you still haven't used it, you've got your answer.

Here's another trick I love when you're on the fence: The 20/20 Rule, originally coined by the Minimalists, says if you could replace the item for less than twenty dollars and in under twenty minutes, let it go.[1] But here's the key: Adjust the numbers to fit your life. Maybe your comfort zone is ten dollars and fifteen minutes. Or thirty dollars and an hour. The point isn't the math; it's the mindset. If something's easy and affordable to replace, you don't need to let it take up prime real estate in your home just in case. Tack this on to the opportunity question. If the answer is no and it falls within your personal version of the 20/20 Rule? That's your green light. That's your reassurance. You're not being wasteful by letting it go—you're being wise.

Assessing your stuff this way is like using a truth serum. It reveals what's quietly taking up space and what's actively supporting your day-to-day life. When you get in the habit of asking this one simple question (and pairing it with a little logic like the 20/20 Rule), the noise starts to clear. You don't need a spreadsheet. You just need to be honest.

4. Choose to Keep, Donate, or Sell It

This is the moment we tend to stall: decision time.

Don't let yourself overthink it. Just choose to keep, donate, or sell. That's it.

- **Keep:** If it's staying, it needs a home. Not a random pile or a vague "for now" spot, but a real, designated place where it belongs. And if you're stuck because the ideal home is full or not quite figured out yet? Give it a temporary, but intentional, landing zone. One you plan to revisit. That's still progress. Clutter happens when things float around without a plan. So claim a spot, even if it's not perfect, and keep moving forward.

- **Donate or Sell:** Donation is the easiest path—low friction, high reward. Selling can work, but only if it doesn't become a whole other project. Ask yourself, *Is it worth the time and energy this will take?* If it is, go for it. If it's not, bless and release. Your time matters more.
- **Time Will Tell Box:** Still stuck? That's okay. Tuck the item away for four to six weeks. Set a reminder. When you open it later, chances are you'll barely remember what's in there—and the choice will feel so much easier.

5. Free Up Headspace by Removing It

This is the part a lot of people skip, not on purpose but out of fatigue. The clutter is in bags and boxes, so it feels done. Until it's out of your house, though, it's not really gone, and it's still taking up mental headspace and energy. You need to complete the decluttering task to get that energy back.

Here's how to follow through like you mean it.

- **Schedule a drop-off.** Don't simply tell yourself you'll do it "sometime soon" or when you "get around to it."

Pick a day and mark your calendar. Treat it like an appointment with your future self.

- **Schedule a pickup.** Check online for local charities or organizations that offer donation pickups. Having a truck on the way is wildly motivating—and it puts a helpful deadline in place so you don't stall out.
- **Move it to your car—now.** Don't set it by the door or in the garage. Get it out of your living space. This one step alone prevents 80 percent of backtracking.
- **Don't reopen the bags.** Seriously, don't. You already made the decision. Reopening is a fast track to second-guessing. Trust the version of yourself who set you on this course.

This is more than just logistics; it's a mindset shift. Finishing what you start builds trust with yourself, so you can think, *I follow through. I finish strong. I make space for what matters.*

And that space you're making is not only physical. It's emotional relief and mental clarity—a clean break from the cycle that used to keep you stuck. After all, the goal here isn't just less stuff. It's having more peace and margin and feeling more fully present in the life you're creating.

The Five Basic Decluttering Steps in a Kitchen

When Laura joined my program, her kitchen felt like a daily battle. The counters were never clear. The drawers were overflowing. The pantry shelves were crammed with half-used ingredients and expired boxes she hadn't touched in years.

"I avoid cooking because it just stresses me out," she admitted.

Here's how she used the five basic decluttering steps to start changing her space.

1. Determine an Item's "Home" and Boundary Lines

"How much is enough?" Laura asked. She settled on one drawer for everyday utensils and one for specialty tools. Pantry items had to fit on the shelf—no more precarious stacks or mystery zones in the back. She didn't have to declutter everything, just stay inside the lines she defined.

2. Identify How It Actively Serves Your Present Life

"What's the purpose of this kitchen?" was the next question. Her answer was simple: "I want it to be easier to cook." That clarity made it easier to say goodbye to the spiralizer she hadn't used in years and the waffle maker she didn't even like using. She wouldn't keep things out of a sense of duty. It was more important to feel alignment with her purpose.

3. Ask If You've Had the Chance to Use It

"Have I had the opportunity to use it in the last six to twelve months?" came next. In the pantry, she checked expiration dates and tossed anything past its prime. In the drawers, she realized she always reached for the same two spatulas. The rest were just taking up space. And for the items she wasn't sure about, she used the 20/20 Rule: If she could replace it for under twenty dollars and in less than twenty minutes, it probably wasn't worth holding on to. That one-two punch—opportunity plus replaceability—helped her get honest and keep moving.

4. Choose to Keep, Donate, or Sell It

From there, she made quick decisions. Broken items were discarded. Duplicates and barely used gadgets went to the donate bin, and she found a local recycling center using Earth911.com. That extra step gave her peace of mind—she was letting go in a way that felt responsible and aligned with her values.

5. Free Up Headspace by Removing It

Laura scheduled her donation drop-off that weekend. She moved the bags to her car and didn't reopen a single box.

Afterward, Laura told me, "I can't believe how much easier cooking is now! My counters are clear, and I feel inspired to try new recipes because I'm not digging through piles of stuff to find what I need."

Are you ready to start trying it in your own home? Before you do, keep in mind you don't need to attack a whole room or the whole house. Zero in on one contained space—one drawer, one shelf, one surface you use every day. Is there one that makes you sigh every time you see it? What if that space could feel done?

Not perfect. Not color-coded. Just functional. Lighter. Yours again.

Pick one small place to start and use your first tool to address it. The five basic decluttering steps will help you build momentum and belief in yourself.

Once you start moving through that outermost layer—making those easier-to-knock-out, low-emotion decisions—you'll start to notice what's underneath. The deeper stuff. The trickier layers. That's where we're headed next.

But don't worry—we've got a tool for that too. Let's go get it.

TAKE ACTION

First, find a place in your home where you could find superficial clutter. Where are some easily overlooked items you may not need—the random everyday stuff that piled up because life got busy?

Next, use the five basic decluttering steps to decide what you want to do. Here they are again with a few reminders and tips.

1. **Determine an item's "home" and boundary lines.** Decide

how much space something gets—then stick to it. A built-in limit simplifies every decision.

2. **Identify how it actively serves your present life.** If it's not supporting your current routines, values, or needs—it's just taking up space. Be honest about what fits your season of life and deserves precious real estate.

3. **Ask if you've had the chance to use it.** Ask, "Have I had the opportunity to use this in the last six to twelve months?" If you've had the opportunity but didn't use it, that's your answer—it can go. If you haven't had the opportunity yet (maybe it's been buried or forgotten), give it one final shot: move it somewhere visible and test it out. If it still doesn't get used, it's time to let it go. You can also create your own version of the 20/20 Rule: If you could replace it for under twenty dollars (or your determined price) and in under twenty minutes (or the time frame you're comfortable with), it's probably safe to release. Adjust the numbers to fit your life—then use it as an extra layer of clarity when you're stuck.

4. **Choose to keep, donate, or sell it.** Make a fast decision. If you *keep* it, give it a clear home. If you *donate* or *sell*, move it to your donation bin or listing pile. If you're not sure, try a Time Will Tell Box and check back in four to six weeks.

5. **Free up headspace by removing it.** Decluttering isn't done until it's gone, and leaving bags by the door keeps you stuck mentally. Schedule your donation drop-off.

Move items to your car now, not later. And don't reopen the bags—you already made the decision.

Remember, you don't need more time. You just need a plan. And now, you've got one. You can do this without overwhelm, overthinking, or burnout. Use it to build momentum, make decisions faster, and start seeing real progress.

Chapter 5

Scarcity Clutter

I once packed four backup outfits for a two-day trip. What if it rained? What if it got cold? What if I spilled coffee on my jeans or decided I suddenly wanted to be a "hat person" halfway through the weekend?

I packed two pairs of shoes for every outfit. (What if I wanted to dress it up?) A scarf I'd never worn but suddenly might need. A jacket that didn't match anything. Four snack options like I was prepping for a trail hike in the Alps instead of a girls' weekend in New York City.

By the time I zipped my suitcase, it looked like I might be moving. You know what ended up happening? I wore exactly what I originally planned. The rest just weighed me down—literally and mentally. Dragging it through the airport. Digging through it to find what I needed. Shoving it all back in at the end of the weekend, annoyed with myself but weirdly convinced I'd need it next time.

When I finally hoisted my suitcase on to the scale at the airport, the weight felt absurd. But also a little familiar. Because I wasn't just packing for a trip. I was trying to protect myself from every possible inconvenience by carrying it all with me.

This is what we do with our stuff at home too.

We keep the broken fan just in case the AC goes out. We save the third set of sheets for the guest bed no one uses, the extra muffin tin, the second set of golf clubs, the stack of appliance manuals from 2008. Not because we use them. But because something inside us whispers, *What if?*

What if I regret this?

What if I can't get it back?

That whisper might sound quiet, but it's powerful. It convinces us to hold on. To overprepare and keep surrounding ourselves with stuff—not because it serves us, but because it soothes our fears.

But here's the catch: That kind of safety is an illusion. The clutter stays. The fear stays. And so does the weight of it all.

This chapter is about pulling the thread tied to your "just-in-case" thinking. Let's take a closer look and see what it's made of so you can begin to loosen the grip it has had on your space, your mind, and your peace.

The Mindset of Scarcity Clutter

You're not alone if this mindset feels familiar. As you might guess from my packing story, it felt familiar to me too.

In chapter 2, we talked about your Stuff Story—the combination of beliefs and experiences that have quietly shaped the way you hold on to things. You probably didn't write that story on purpose. You inherited it, absorbed it, or pieced it together from the people and seasons that formed you.

For me, one of those voices belonged to my grandmother. She saved everything—jars, twist ties, fabric scraps, even those little closure tabs from bread bags. Her motto was simple: "You never know when it might come in handy."

The younger version of me never questioned this. It was just what she did. Looking back now, I can see that her habits weren't simply based on thriftiness. They were rooted in survival. Not having enough was a reality in her lifetime. And even though I didn't live through the same hardships, I internalized her mindset like it was mine to carry.

You probably have personal influences like this too.

There are also cultural influences we're all feeling. The fear of not having enough is everywhere—you're not imagining it. It's baked into our world. Ads constantly remind us what we're missing. Social media highlight reels show "well-stocked" homes and picture-perfect pantries. Influencers and podcasters tell us to "stock up while it's on sale" or "grab extras just in case."

And so we do.

We hold on to the backup coffee maker or shelf of skincare products we didn't end up liking but felt too guilty to toss. We're not using them, but we're afraid we might need them later. We worry we won't be able to afford a replacement. Or we tell ourselves, "There's nothing wrong with it. Maybe someday I'll use it."

But here's the thing: Holding on to more doesn't make you more prepared. It makes you more overwhelmed.

This isn't about swinging to the opposite extreme of hyperminimalism or ignoring financial realities. It's about finding harmony—your version of enough. The kind that reflects your values, your season of life, your peace of mind. There's freedom in recognizing when fear is trying to drive your decision-making and learning to trust that you have enough already.

For you, that mindset might have come from a parent who never threw anything away. Or a culture that treats preparedness like morality. Or your own lived experience, from times when there truly wasn't enough.

Wherever it came from, the result is the same: You can end up holding on to things not because you love or use them, but because you're afraid of what might happen if you don't.

That fear feels protective, but most of the time, it's not keeping you safe. It's keeping you stuck.

The 4 *S*'s Framework

Imagine yourself standing frozen in front of an old cell phone charger or pair of jeans you haven't worn in years, staring and wondering, *What if I need this later?* In that moment you don't need more willpower. You need a pattern interruption. A way to get out of your head and into action. That's where this next tool comes in.

I call it the 4 *S*'s Framework, and it was born out of my own frustration. Every time I tried to declutter, I got stuck in the same loop of indecision, so I created a simple process to jump out of that and keep moving forward. This framework was inspired in part by a coaching concept I first heard years ago from Corinne Crabtree, who used a similar

4-step model—her "4 N's"—to help women overcome self-doubt around weight loss.[1] While my version is different and focused on decluttering, I love how she used a clear mental structure to navigate stuck points, and it planted a seed. Both of our approaches are rooted in cognitive-behavioral therapy (CBT), and this tool helps you untangle fear-based thoughts, reframe them with truth, and move forward one tiny decision at a time. There will be no giant purge here. No guilt or shame either. Just gentle, grounded confidence.

Spot It

The first step is simply noticing the fear-based thinking without judgment or trying to solve it right away. As we've said, these are questions like, *What if I need this someday?* What if I regret letting it go? What if I can't replace it later? Shine a flashlight on the script that's been quietly running in the background—because you can't shift what you haven't spotted.

It might sound like your voice, but it's often someone else's. It was passed down from a parent, shaped by hard times, or reinforced by a culture obsessed with "what if." This doesn't make the fear silly or wrong; it means it's been sitting there unchecked, guiding your choices in ways you didn't realize.

Spotting it brings it into the light. And once it's in the light, you can do something with it.

In one published study researchers found that people are more likely to hold on to items if they're asked to imagine future regret before deciding to let go.[2] Just the act of imagining a potential "what if" was enough to derail confident decisions.

Sound familiar?

That's the kind of mental loop you can interrupt, shifting from future-fear to present truth.

Soften It

Once you've spotted the fear, don't bulldoze it. Meet it with compassion.

Reactive thoughts like, *You should hang on to this, just in case,* aren't trying to sabotage you. They're trying to protect you. The problem is, they're functioning as pressure, which becomes an obstacle that ultimately weighs you down.

So instead of shaming yourself for feeling hesitant or silly or stuck, make room for grace. Try thinking, *Of course I feel this way. Of course I'm nervous to let go. Of course I'm trying to avoid regret.*

You don't have to erase the fear. Just soften your grip on it so it can loosen its grip on you. You're allowed to feel the fear and still move forward. When you respond to it with gentleness instead of judgment, you create the space to do that.

Shift It

This is the part where the inner dialogue starts to change. You've noticed the fear. You've softened it. Now it's time to reframe it. Think of this not as toxic positivity or false confidence but as a nudge toward truth.

These subtle shifts are powerful. The more you practice them, the more you prove to yourself that fear doesn't get the final say. You do.

Instead of:	**Try:**
What if I regret this?	This item already served its purpose. If I need it again, I trust myself to find a solution.
But it still works . . .	Just because it's useful doesn't mean it's useful to me.
Keeping this makes me prepared.	Keeping this makes me overwhelmed, and I'm allowed to want peace more than backup plans.

Step Forward

This is where mindset meets movement. You don't need to overhaul a whole closet or dump every box in the garage. You just need one small step that says, *I trust myself.*

That might look like:

- letting go of one "just-in-case" item you've been hanging on to for years;
- dropping a donation bag into your trunk instead of your hallway;

- writing down another item you already own that does the same job as the thing you're debating letting go of.

Small steps are not second best. They're how real change begins, especially with scarcity clutter. Every time you act, even in a tiny way, you're doing something important: You're teaching your brain that you're capable. You're reminding your body what relief feels like. You're choosing trust over fear. And the more you step forward, the easier it gets to do it again.

Reframing Your Thoughts and Attachments

The third part of the 4 *S*'s Framework—Shift It—is especially key because it's where we change the stories we tell ourselves. We keep the cracked cooler or the extra spatula not because we love them but because of what we believe they're protecting us from.

Let's take a closer look at a few of the most common fears and what it might sound like to gently reframe them.

What if I need this someday?

This single question kept me holding on to tangled cords, half-functioning fans, and mystery kitchen parts for years. I thought I was being prepared. But the truth was, I wasn't trusting my resourcefulness to find what I needed if the time ever came.

I remember finally letting go of a bulky fan I was keeping for a hypothetical air-conditioning breakdown. I told myself, *If that ever happens, I'll borrow one. Or find a replacement that fits my life then. Until that day, I don't need this fan taking up my space.*

What if I regret letting it go?

Sometimes regret shows up not because we loved the item, but because we meant to use it. It represents a plan we didn't follow through on, or an identity we wanted to step into.

Maybe I'll start batch cooking.

Maybe I'll use this when life slows down.

When that version of life never comes, the regret creeps in.

Reframe it like this: *I'm not failing by letting this go—I'm accepting what's real right now.*

When I let go of a slow cooker I hadn't touched in years, I reminded myself, *Owning it never made me use it. Keeping it won't either.* I was allowed to release the pressure and reclaim the space.

It feels wasteful to get rid of it.

Letting go of something that's technically "still good" can feel wasteful. But holding on to it doesn't make it less wasteful; it just makes it your burden.

Reframe it like this: Releasing this item lets it be useful to someone else.

When I let go of kitchen tools, I wasn't tossing value; I was passing it on. They could sit unused in my drawer—or someone else could benefit from them.

But this cost money!

Ah, money guilt. This one runs deep. But here's what I had to learn: Keeping something doesn't refund the money. And letting it go doesn't mean you failed; it means you're learning.

I've told myself this so many times: *I already paid for the lesson. Now I get to create space for what I truly need.*

Each time you reframe one of these fears, you're doing more than decluttering a drawer. You're retraining your brain to believe a new story: You'll be okay without the "just in case." You're capable of figuring it out when the time comes. And you don't need to be ruled by fear to be safe, smart, or prepared.

Once you start embracing that new story, the clutter will begin to lose its grip.

Now let me show you what that looks like in real life.

Kendra's Story: Finding Freedom Through the 4 *S*'s

Kendra's garage was overflowing with old sports equipment, half-finished crafts and craft supplies, and bins labeled "random cords." She admitted she wasn't ready to toss most of it (because "you never know"). When Kendra and I first talked about her clutter, her frustration was palpable.

"It's not just stuff," she said. "Every time I see it, I feel like I'm letting my family down because I can't keep it together."

The clutter wasn't reflecting an inability to manage a home. It was reflecting the fears and beliefs Kendra had been carrying for years. Together, we worked through the 4 *S*'s Framework to help her break free.

Spot It

Kendra started by noticing the fears that kept coming up. She realized that her "what if" thoughts had taken on a life of their own. *What if the kids need this equipment again someday?*

What if I regret letting it go and we end up having to buy it again? What if I get rid of something and it turns out to be a mistake?

These thoughts weren't just about the items—they were tied to a deeper fear of being unprepared or making the wrong decision.

"It's easier to just keep it all than to deal with the possibility of regret," she reasoned.

Soften It

Instead of beating herself up, Kendra practiced self-compassion. She reminded herself, *Of course I feel this way—keeping things feels safer. But that doesn't mean I need to keep everything.*

She realized she wasn't alone in feeling this way and that her fears didn't make her weak or incapable; they made her human. She also gave herself permission to move at her own pace, knowing that letting go could happen on her own timeline.

Shift It

Next, Kendra began reframing her thoughts.

For the old sports equipment, she told herself, *It served its purpose, and now it can go to someone else who will use it.*

For the half-finished craft supplies, she thought, *These represent a season of my life that has passed. I want to make room for the life I'm living now.*

These reframes didn't erase her fears entirely, but they helped her approach the process with a sense of control and clarity. She started to see her items not as burdens but as opportunities to decide what would stay and what she was ready to release.

Step Forward

Kendra's next move wasn't all-or-nothing. For some items—like the duplicate camping chair, the broken scooter, and the collection of mystery charging cords—she felt clear and confident. She let them go on the spot.

But for others—like her kids' outgrown sports gear and a box of kitchen backups—she still wasn't sure. So her step forward for those items became creating a Time Will

Tell Box. She labeled it with the date, tucked everything inside, and set a reminder to revisit it in six weeks.

"Setting up the Time Will Tell Box felt like giving myself a safety net," she said. "It made the decision feel less permanent."

During those six weeks, Kendra didn't think about the items in the box. When the time came to revisit it, she realized she hadn't touched a single thing.

"It was such a relief to see that I didn't need any of it. Letting it go didn't feel hard anymore. It felt freeing."

After clearing out her garage, Kendra said something else that stuck with me.

"It's not just the space that feels lighter to me. I'm lighter too. I finally feel like I'm in control, not my stuff."

That shift wasn't only about the clutter; it was about proving to herself that she could handle uncertainty. Kendra had spent years believing that keeping everything was the safer choice, but now she was starting to trust herself in a way she hadn't before.

Months later, Kendra told me something that caught me off guard in the best way. "The other day, I was at Target holding this set of mixing bowls," she said. "And I actually heard that old voice in my head whispering, *You might need these someday.* But this time, I smiled, put them back, and thought, *I've got this.*"

That's the real win. Not just less clutter, but more trust.

Mindset work is ongoing; it's not something you do once and then check off a list. Think of it like strengthening a muscle: The more you challenge your beliefs and take small actions, the quieter those "what-if" voices become.

Letting Go Is a Skill—Not a Personality Trait

If you're anything like Kendra and me, you've been trying to make decisions with fear on one side of the scale—and nothing on the other. Of course fear has been dominating; it has gone unchallenged!

But now you've got a tool for putting weight—the weight of clarity and trust—on the other side of the scale, and it's going to tip the balance.

The 4 *S*'s don't make your fears disappear. They don't erase uncertainty. They help guide you when "what if" feels loud and letting go feels risky. Each time you spot a fear, soften your response, shift the thought, and take one small step forward, you add weight to that scale so you can counterbalance fear with freedom. And over time that side starts to win.

Each time you spot a fear, soften your response, shift the thought, and take one small step forward.

This isn't just about a garage or a drawer. It's about building momentum for the life you want to live, one that isn't tethered to "someday" or stalled by "just in case." Let this chapter be your turning point. The moment you stop organizing your fears and start clearing space for your actual life. The moment you realize you're not stuck—you're just one small, confident step away from momentum.

You're already on your way.

REFLECT

- What in your home could be considered scarcity clutter?
- How is your mindset around scarcity clutter tied to your Stuff Story? What influenced it most?
- Can you recall any critical thoughts you might have had about yourself when you're responding to fear? For example, perhaps you struggle to trust your future self to be resourceful.
- What are some more compassionate words you could practice saying to yourself instead? For example, *I've found ways to take care of myself for years. I'll be able to do it in the future too.*

TAKE ACTION

Pick a spot in your home where you have scarcity clutter. Then use the 4 *S*'s Framework to quiet the "what-ifs" and take small, confident steps forward.

Spot It: Notice a fear-based thought when it pops up. *What if I need this someday? What if I regret letting it go?* Don't judge it—just pause and shine a light on it. Naming it is the first step to loosening its grip.

Soften It: Respond to the fear with compassion, not criticism. *Of course I feel this way. I'm trying to protect myself.* You're not weak or silly; you're human. Kindness will weaken the fear.

Shift It: Reframe the thought with something more helpful. Instead of, *But it still works*, try, *It's not working for me.* Instead of, *Keeping this makes me prepared*, try, *It's actually making me overwhelmed.* These small shifts tip the scales toward clarity and trust.

Step Forward: Take one small action. Let go of one "just-in-case" item. Write down a backup you already own. Or put uncertain items in a Time Will Tell Box. Every step forward builds momentum and builds your belief that you can do this.

Chapter 6

Sentimental Clutter

I'm just too sentimental. I could never let this stuff go."

Have you ever said that? Or heard it from someone else?

Maybe the clutter in your home drives you a little nuts, but every time you try to follow that well-meaning advice to just toss it, you hit a wall. It doesn't feel light or freeing. It feels like you're ripping out pieces of your story.

If you've ever felt that way, you're someone who cares deeply. And honestly? That's not a weakness. That's human. If you've ever felt that way, it doesn't mean you're too emotional or too attached—it means you've got a big heart. The problem isn't that you're too sentimental; it's that no one ever gave you a way to declutter that honors how much these things mean to you.

This chapter is all about addressing sentimental clutter—those items that hold meaning, memories, milestones. When something holds meaning, letting go feels bigger than just tossing an object; it can feel like erasing part of who you are. So instead of trying to force yourself to be ruthless, I want to give you a new tool in this chapter. A new lens. A better approach. One that allows you to let go when you're ready and hold on when it still matters.

Let's start with a story.

One day, a professor walked into his classroom holding up a weathered leather bag. It had scuffed corners, worn straps, and the kind of patina that only comes from years of use. You could have walked past this raggedy thing at a thrift store without a second glance.

"How much would you pay for this?" he asked his students.

A few hands shot up.

"Ten dollars."

"Maybe thirty, if it's real leather."

"Zero dollars—I wouldn't buy it."

To them, it was just an old bag. Used, ordinary, forgettable.

Then, the professor dimmed the lights and played a short video. It told the story of a young boy whose father had gone off to war. Letters became their bridge—his father's voice on paper, filled with stories, hope, and reminders that the boy was loved and missed.

Those letters were everything to the boy. He read them over and over, then folded each one carefully and tucked them into a leather bag—this leather bag.

He carried that bag everywhere. To school. To the treehouse. Even to bed. It held not only letters but love and hope. It was holding him together.

When his father finally came home, the boy—now grown—still had the bag. When the video ended, the professor held it up once more.

"Now," he asked quietly, "how much would you pay for this bag?"

The room was still. Silent, apart from some sniffles. A few students wiped their cheeks.

Someone finally whispered, "It's priceless."

The bag had new meaning. It was still scuffed-up leather and stitching, but it now held something far more powerful—the weight of a boy's longing and a father's love. The ache of distance and the hope of return. That dingy bag was a vessel of memory, story, and connection.

That's what our sentimental items are too. They become love in tangible form, a sacred stand-in for the people and moments that have shaped us. We look at them and remember who we were, who we loved, and what we never want to forget.

Having Emotional Ties Is Normal

Maybe you have a bundle of old T-shirts that remind you of college, even though you never wear them. Or a bridesmaid dress from your best friend's wedding that marked a meaningful season. You might have your grandmother's china set collecting dust in storage, but the idea of getting rid of it feels wrong.

As we've said, being sentimental is human. It's a sign of strength and deep emotional connection—to people, to memories, to moments that shaped you. There's nothing wrong with that.

The question to wrestle with is, What do you want to do with those meanings now?

Many of the women I work with say things like, "I know I shouldn't keep all this stuff, but I can't help it." There's a sense that caring about physical items means they're failing at simplifying or meeting minimalist standards. But here's what I want you to hear: You don't have to stop feeling deeply in order to declutter.

You can declutter without feeling heartless because the goal isn't to erase your past or discard every sentimental item you own. I'm not here to tell you to toss your grandma's handwritten letters or your dad's favorite hat.

In fact, I still have a small box of sentimental things that mean the world to me. There's a handful of cards from each of my family members, a stack of printed photos from childhood, and a few keepsakes I only look at a couple times a year—but every time I do, they bring me a deep sense of joy. They've earned their place. They're not clutter; they're connection.

I'll be honest: I used to feel a lot of pressure to digitize all of it. All the experts seemed to agree that scanning your photos and cards was the "right" thing to do to save space, simplify, and modernize. But there are a few dozen physical photos that felt too special to reduce to pixels on a screen. Holding them in my hands . . . seeing the wear and tear of time . . . that was part of the magic for me.

There's no one-size-fits-all "right" way to handle

sentimental clutter. Your approach might look different from mine. You may want to digitize. You may not. You may want to display something proudly on a shelf or tuck it into a box you revisit every December.

What matters is that it feels right to you. You can keep things with intention, not out of duty or fear. You can release what no longer serves you and honor what still does. And you get to approach all of it in your own unique way.

And because I hope you feel you can do the same while reading this book, I'll mention that we'll be referencing scenarios of loss in this chapter. If that subject matter feels too tender to you right now, give yourself margin and good care. You can always revisit this when you're ready.

Sentimental Clutter Versus Guilt Clutter

Let's clear something up right away: Not everything you think is sentimental truly is. Sometimes duty puts on a sentimental mask. These are the gifts, heirlooms, or keepsakes you hold on to because you think you *should*, not because they spark real connection or joy. The idea of getting rid of them feels wrong, like you'd be letting someone down.

I see this all the time with my students. They'll say, "I

can't let this go—it was a gift." Or, "This belonged to my grandmother, so I have to keep it."

But when they slow down and really look at it, the story changes. They're not keeping the item because it lights them up. They're keeping it because they'd feel guilty if they didn't.

Take my student Kara. She had a vase she inherited after her grandmother passed. It was beautiful, but not at all her style. "It doesn't even match anything in my house," she admitted. "I have other things from Grandma that I actually love. But what if I let go of it and then my mom asks about it someday?"

That's the tricky part about guilt clutter: It sounds like love or duty. But really, it's a form of self-protection. We hang on to items out of fear—fear of hurting someone's feelings, of judgment, of what it means to let something go.

But here's the truth: Keeping something out of guilt isn't the same as honoring it. And it's not the same as honoring the person who gave it to you either.

When Kara realized that holding on to that vase wasn't adding meaning or happiness to her life, she was able to start releasing it with peace. She told herself, *I still have other things that remind me of my grandma. I don't need to keep everything to keep the connection.*

Curating Versus Collecting: Honoring What Matters Most

Sometimes you've got a bundle of sentimental clutter in front of you—a mug from a vacation you barely remember as well as a bracelet your husband gave you in your dating days. Clearly, not all sentimental items are created equal. Some things tug at your heartstrings a little, while others hold part of your story with profound, irreplaceable meaning.

But when everything feels sentimental or "special," nothing truly is. When each item seems too meaningful to part with—every birthday card, every concert T-shirt, every kindergarten art project—you can lose sight of what truly matters. What once held joy becomes a jumble of pressure, guilt, and decision fatigue.

Here's a question for you: What if you saw yourself not as a collector but as a curator? A collector gathers everything; a curator selects with intention. She picks out the pieces that best tell the story, preserve the heart of a moment, and reflect legacy, memory, and meaning—without the overwhelm.

That shift alone can bring so much clarity.

Take my student Olivia. She had five large bins of her kids' baby clothes packed away in the attic, and every time she thought about decluttering them, she froze. "What if I regret it later?" she asked. "What if they want these someday?"

Together, we reframed it.

Instead of feeling pressure to keep everything to preserve the memories, she decided to curate. And as a starting point? She set a clear boundary—one small box per child. (Remember the Five Basic Decluttering Steps from chapter 4 and how the first step was setting boundaries? That same approach works well with sentimental clutter too.)

She chose their first baby shoes, a hospital onesie, and one special outfit from a favorite family photo. The rest, she released with peace.

Later she told me, "The bins felt like a burden, but these boxes feel like a gift. I can actually enjoy them now, and one day, so will my kids."

Curating isn't about minimizing your memories. It's about elevating and amplifying them. When you let go of the excess, the things that matter most have more space to shine.

The ART Framework

Some items are simply too wrapped in meaning to declutter with a quick decision. These aren't the "vase from Grandma that isn't my style" pieces. These are the handwritten letters, the wedding dress, the keepsakes from someone you've loved and lost. For those, you need something gentler and more intentional.

That's where the ART (Ask, Repurpose, Time) Framework comes in. It will guide you in evaluating the things that tug hardest at your heart.

Ask

Before you decide what to do with a sentimental item, ask a few questions.

- Why have I kept this?
- What does it represent for me?
- Does it have the same meaning it used to, or has that meaning shifted over time?

Sometimes just naming the reason we've held on to something is enough to bring clarity. You realize you haven't let it go because it reminds you of a person or place. Or you're afraid that releasing it would mean forgetting. But often, the memory lives in you—not in the item.

A study from Pennsylvania State University found that people who photographed sentimental items before parting with them were significantly more likely to let them go.[1] Why? Because it helped them preserve the meaning without needing to hold on to the object. It's a small act that can make a big emotional difference.

Repurpose

Not everything has to be displayed or be useful in a conventional way. If an item is meaningful to you, consider how it might still serve a purpose or how it might be transformed to bring more joy.

For example, my student Karen had a box full of her mother's handwritten recipe cards, some with little notes in the margins, others smudged with flour from decades of family baking. Karen loved them, but they were tucked away in storage, and she rarely saw them.

"They mean so much to me," she said, "but I feel disconnected from them when they're sitting in a bin."

So we found a simple way to bring them into her life.

Karen selected a handful of her mom's favorite recipes—ones they had made together or that reminded her of home—and had them framed. She hung them in her kitchen, right above her baking counter.

"Now I see them every day," she told me later. "They don't just remind me of her; they inspire me to keep the tradition going."

By giving those recipes a place of honor, Karen not only preserved her mom's memory but also brought it forward, into her present life.

Karen's story is a powerful reminder that sentimental items don't always need to be boxed away or reinvented to be meaningful. Sometimes, a small act of intention—like giving something a place of honor—can breathe new life into a memory.

If you're looking for simple ways to do the same, here are a few ideas to inspire you:

- Turn old T-shirts from memorable events into a quilt you can cozy up with.
- Create a shadow box with small keepsakes like concert tickets, dried flowers, or medals that mark important milestones.
- Display one or two meaningful items—like a piece of jewelry or a trophy—on a shelf or mantel, instead of storing a whole collection.

None of this is about creating a museum. It's about integrating your memories into your life in ways that feel thoughtful, personal, and true to you.

But let me say this clearly: You don't have to repurpose everything. If you want to keep your grandmother's letters in a box and read them once a year with a cup of tea—that's enough. These things don't need to be displayed or "useful" to be worthy.

Time

Sometimes you feel torn considering what to do with an item, and the fact is, you're just not ready. The grief is too fresh. The emotions too raw. The meaning too heavy to sort through right away. In those moments, time becomes the most compassionate tool in your toolbox.

When my student Sarah lost her mother, she couldn't part with a single item. Every dish towel, every trinket, every knickknack felt like a thread holding her to her mother's memory.

We used the Time Will Tell Box—a familiar tool by now, but powerful in a new way here.

She packed away the items she wasn't ready to make decisions about and set a reminder for six months later. When that day came, she found clarity she hadn't expected. Some things she let go of with peace. Others—like her mom's handwritten recipe cards—stayed.

Sarah bundled them with a soft ribbon and placed them in a small wooden box on her counter. It wasn't about display; it was about presence. Every time she reached for a measuring cup or brewed her morning coffee, that box reminded her of her mom's quiet warmth and all the meals they had shared. It was storage, but also connection.

When time isn't a luxury—say you're clearing out a loved

one's home on a deadline—know that grace still applies. Focus on what feels most meaningful in the moment. You can always revisit the rest. Take your own path to honoring your emotions, your memories, and your readiness.

Using the ART Framework

After Taylor's dad passed away, she found herself with an entire room filled with his belongings—tools, books, clothes, and a collection of trinkets he'd gathered over the years. Every time she stepped inside, she felt a flood of emotion. A heavy question hung in the air: *How can I possibly let go of these things? It feels like I'm letting go of him.*

So Taylor and I turned to the ART Framework—not as a quick fix but as a compassionate guide.

- **Ask:** Taylor started by gently asking herself what each item meant to her. When she looked at her dad's extensive tool collection, she realized the connection wasn't emotional; it was dutiful. "I don't even know how to use half of these," she admitted. The tools had become a stand-in for her grief, not a reflection of their relationship. Once she named that, it became easier to release them—with peace instead of guilt.
- **Repurpose:** Some things, however, did feel deeply meaningful. Taylor chose to keep his cuff links and had them framed alongside a photo of the two of them fishing. That small, intentional display now

hangs in her hallway, where it catches the light, draws her eye, and brings her comfort on even the hardest days. "It's like having a piece of him with me," she said. "But it doesn't weigh me down."

- **Time:** There were still a few items she wasn't ready to decide on, like his fishing gear. It held memories that felt too fresh to sort through. So we used the Time Will Tell Box, giving her space instead of pressure. After some time, with a bit more distance and clarity, she opened the box again. While she still didn't feel ready to let go of all the fishing supplies, she chose to gift some of the gear to a family friend who had always admired it and shared her dad's love of the water. "It felt like I was giving it a second life," she told me. "And I know he would've loved that."

Taylor didn't keep everything. She didn't need to. What she did keep was chosen with care. And that's the heart of the ART Framework—it helps you move from overwhelmed to intentional, from stuck in grief to grounded in love.

You don't need to hold on to everything to honor the past. Just hold on to what holds you, whatever makes your heart sing.

I know this work can feel tender. You might feel like you're peeling back layers you didn't expect to find or sitting with emotions you thought you'd already processed. That's okay.

You don't have to rush it. Just keep showing up with honesty, curiosity, and care. Every time you pause to reflect, choose to keep what matters, and release what doesn't, you're not only making space in your home. You're honoring your story.

And I promise—there's even more lightness, peace, and freedom waiting on the other side.

REFLECT

Think about an item that may or may not be truly sentimental clutter—it could be clutter you're keeping out of duty. Try answering these questions.

- If I weren't feeling guilty about the idea of letting go of this, would I still want it?
- Do I love it, or just feel obligated to keep it?
- Does it make my space feel more like me, or more like someone else?

Recognizing the difference between guilt and genuine sentimentality is one of the most freeing steps in this process.

TAKE ACTION

Find an item of deeply sentimental clutter, and then move through the simple, gentle guide of the ART Framework.

Ask: Get curious about your connection.

- Why have I kept this?
- What does it represent to me?

- Is it still serving that same purpose—or has that shifted?

Sometimes naming the meaning helps loosen the grip. The item might be holding a memory—but the memory lives in you.

Repurpose: Honor it your way.

- Could it be displayed? Framed? Woven into daily life with intention?
- Or does it simply belong in a curated keepsake box you revisit once in a while?

Repurposing doesn't mean productivity; it means presence. You get to choose what feels most meaningful.

Time: Give yourself permission to not know yet.

- Use a Time Will Tell Box when you're unsure.
- Set a reminder to revisit in a few months—grief and clarity both need room to breathe.

You're not being indecisive—you're being kind to your future self. Sometimes space is the most generous gift you can give.

Let the ART Framework be your guide as you edit your story with care. You don't have to keep everything to honor what matters most; you just need to choose with love.

Chapter 7

Identity Clutter

It started with a pair of running shoes on a shelf and a stack of cookbooks in my kitchen. They weren't in the way. They weren't messy. But every time I saw them, something stirred. There was a twinge of guilt along with a passing thought: *Why didn't you do it?*

The shoes were more than just shoes. They reminded me of when I'd declared to myself: *I'm going to run a marathon*. But a race never happened. And the longer those shoes sat untouched, the more energy they drained from me. Each time they caught my eye, I wrestled with their message: *You haven't followed through*.

Then there were the cookbooks. Beautifully bound, filled with pages I had never once cooked from. I had collected them with a vision of hosting elegant dinner parties, gliding through the kitchen like a modern-day Martha Stewart. I'd grown up watching her on TV, imagining that one day I'd become that kind of woman. Graceful. Effortless. Master of soufflés.

Spoiler alert: I never became that woman.

I honestly didn't even want to become that woman.

But I hadn't admitted that to myself yet. So the books stayed, and like the shoes, they whispered, *You're falling short*.

I used to think I kept things only if they were useful or brought me joy. In truth, I was holding on to items as if they were proof that I could still become the person I once thought I needed to be.

Letting them go felt like I'd be waving the white flag on becoming who I should have become. Admitting that some dreams had changed. Acknowledging that some versions of me weren't coming back. These weren't just objects; they were identity clutter.

Identity clutter is the kind of clutter tied to your self-image—who you were, who you hoped to become, or who you, or others, expected you to be. And here's the thing: It's sneaky. Because it's not just about what you own. It's about what you believe you should want, even when you don't anymore.

Why It's So Hard to Let Go—Even When You Know You Should

Ever notice how something becomes harder to part with just because it's yours? That's not a character flaw. That's psychology.

It's called the *endowment effect*, and it's a bias that causes us to place a higher value on something simply because we own it.[1] Your brain says, *If it's mine, it must be important*. Suddenly that old textbook from college or that unworn blazer for your "someday job" feels indispensable. The fact that it is not useful to you feels irrelevant.

Knowing this gives you an edge; now, you can challenge the thought. You can ask, *If I didn't already own this, would I still choose it today?*

Pondering that question is like turning on a light switch. It helps you see your identity clutter not through the lens of guilt, nostalgia, or expectation, but through clarity, freedom, and honesty.

Once I started asking that question, I saw it everywhere—not only in myself, but in every woman I worked with. Our homes weren't just filled with stuff; they were filled with stories about our identity. And it showed up in three distinct ways.

The Three Types of Identity Clutter

The three types of identity clutter are tied to versions of ourselves. First, let's go back in time.

Who You Used to Be

Identity clutter tied to *who you used to be* is made up of things from past versions of yourself—roles you've outgrown, lifestyles you've shifted out of, seasons you've moved on from. They could be a closet full of business suits from a career you've left behind; musical instruments you haven't played in years; trophies, awards, or certificates that no longer reflect your current values or direction.

These items once made perfect sense. They told the story of who you were, maybe even who you needed to be at that time. But now? They might be more about the identity you've outgrown than the one you're living today.

And here's where it gets tricky: Letting go can feel like betrayal, like you're abandoning that past self.

If you feel that, you can ask, *What if releasing those items is a way to honor her?* Maybe you could be telling her, *You were important. You helped me become who I am today. And I don't need the proof anymore.*

There's grief in that kind of growth. And there's grace. We are not meant to stay the same. And the proof of our becoming doesn't live in storage bins—it lives in us.

Who You Hope to Become

Second, aspirational identity clutter is made up of all the things you thought would help you become a "better" version of yourself—the fitter, healthier, more accomplished, more creative you. It's the collection of planners you swore you'd use to get your life together, the stationary bike you now use as a coatrack, the stack of French cookbooks that looked great on the shelf but never made it to your kitchen counter.

Some of these items serve us. Others quietly shame us.

Aspirational clutter can masquerade as hope, but often it's rooted in comparison or self-judgment. Instead of helping you grow into a version of yourself that feels exciting and true, it subtly suggests you're not enough as you are. Over time, those objects stop seeming like signs of possibilities and start feeling like proof you're falling short.

So how do you tell the difference between something aspirational and something that's just clutter? Ask yourself: *Does this feel like an invitation or an obligation?*

If it inspires you, it belongs. If it burdens you, it doesn't. Look for these signs that the item supports your current self and values:

- You actively engage with it, even if imperfectly.
- It feels like an invitation, not a judgment.
- It aligns with your real values and energy, not a fantasy version of you.

Maybe you have a high-quality yoga mat you roll out once or twice a week. It serves your real life, not an ideal, imaginary one.

But that juicer you bought during your wellness era that now makes you sigh every time you open the cabinet? That's not helping you move forward; it's holding you back. When something becomes a symbol of what you "should" be doing, it's guilting you, not motivating you. And guilt is not a growth strategy.

Who Others Expect You to Be

Clutter tied to who you are expected to be is often the sneakiest because it was never really yours to begin with. It's the stuff you keep because of external expectations—gifts you feel guilty donating, heirlooms you never liked but feel obligated to preserve, clothes that reflect someone else's idea of who you should be. Maybe it's your aunt's expensive artwork you've never liked, collecting dust in a closet; the books from your former mentor you've never felt compelled to read; or the church dress you bought that never truly felt like you.

These items aren't about your past or your goals; they're about expectations. What you were taught to value. How others wanted you to show up. What you were "supposed" to become. This kind of clutter feels tangled in *shoulds* and shame. It's not just hard to let go of—it's hard to even recognize as clutter, because it often comes cloaked in love, tradition, or social pressure.

Even so, these things are loaded with obligation, and that obligation is heavy. And the truth is, you don't have to carry someone else's version of you. You get to choose what aligns with your life now. You define your values, your joy, and your identity.

When we release the things that reflect someone else's story, we make more space to fully live our own. That's a story worth keeping.

So how do we untangle what's truly meaningful from what's weighing us down? I'll show you the questions that helped me do just that.

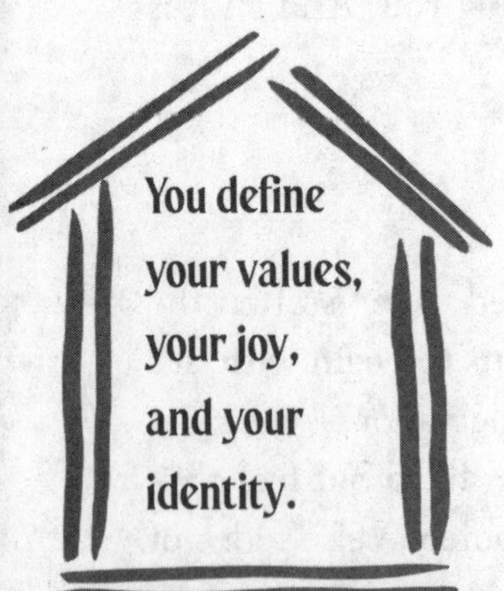

Story, Season, Self

Asking "Do I use this?" or "Does this spark joy?" never got me far with identity clutter. Those questions were too surface-level, too simple for the complex web of stories, expectations, and unspoken hopes tangled up in the items I struggled to part with.

So I began asking different questions—deeper ones that could help me sift through the emotional noise and get to the heart of what was worth keeping. I call them the Story, Season, Self questions.

- **Story:** What story have I tied to this item? Is it a story I still want to live?
- **Season:** Is this item relevant to the season of life I'm in now?
- **Self:** Does this item align with who I am today or who I'm actively becoming?

These questions gave me what so many of us are desperate for when we're stuck in indecision: clarity and compassion. They helped me release not only stuff, but the emotional weight it carried with it. Let me show you what that looked like.

Take the aspirational Martha Stewart cookbooks. Here's how I worked through them using the Story, Season, Self questions.

Story: "What story have I tied to this item? Is it a story I still want to live?"

Every time I saw those cookbooks, I envisioned a version of myself that didn't exist: a woman who joyfully whipped up gourmet meals, her kids happily helping in perfectly matching aprons. I pictured dinner parties straight out of a magazine—candles glowing, place settings just so, laughter echoing through a spotless kitchen. Guests would rave, "How do you do it all?" and I'd smile modestly, like it was no big deal. This woman had it all together.

But I wasn't her. And deep down, I knew it.

The truth was, I didn't want to roast a duck or master soufflés. Cooking, for me, wasn't joyful or elegant—it was a daily scramble to get something (anything!) on the table before someone melted down or the pasta boiled over. And yet, those cookbooks stayed as props in a story I thought I was supposed to live. A story that said being a good mom or a good wife meant being a good cook. That your worth could be measured in made-from-scratch meals and Pinterest-worthy hosting.

And here's the sneaky part: I never actually decided I wanted that story. I absorbed it. From the shows I watched, the pages of homemaking magazines on my mom's coffee table, the unspoken messages about what "success" and "womanhood" looked like. I didn't even realize how heavy that story had become until I started questioning why I was still holding on to it.

Those cookbooks weren't feeding my family; they were feeding my insecurity. Letting them go involved untangling a belief I'd been carrying for years: that I needed to be someone else in order to be enough.

Season: "Is this relevant to the season of life I'm in now?"

The answer was clear but still hard to admit. My days were a blur of school pickups, spilled milk, work deadlines, and refereeing sibling squabbles while stirring pasta with one hand and checking email with the other. I wasn't casually flipping through recipes in a sun-drenched kitchen. I was googling "easy 15-minute meals" at 5:37 p.m. with a toddler attached to my leg. This wasn't a season of soufflés; it was a season of survival.

Yet, every time I saw those cookbooks, I felt the gap between the life I had and the life I imagined. The one where I had more time, more energy, more margin. That different, slower season might come someday, but it wasn't here now.

Have you been there? Feeling the tension of what is and what could be? Struggling to acknowledge some things will have to wait to be explored? Forgetting that seasons, by nature, are meant to come and go? When we're in that place, we need reminding that it's okay for our homes—and our expectations—to change with the seasons.

Letting go of those cookbooks wasn't about giving up on beauty or creativity in the kitchen. It was about releasing a version of life that didn't fit this moment. It was about telling the truth about what I needed right now.

In that moment, what I needed was simplicity. Flexibility. Margin. Not another reminder of a life I wasn't living.

Self: "Does this align with who I am today—or who I truly want to become?"

When I got really honest, the answer hit hard—not in a shameful way, but in a freeing one. I didn't want to become the woman those cookbooks represented. I had just thought I should.

For so long, I'd carried this belief that "real women" knew how to host with ease. That if I could master the perfect dinner party or roast the perfect chicken, I'd finally feel like I had it together and be worthy of admiration, or maybe acceptance. But that version of me wasn't real.

The me I wanted to honor was already showing up—in flour-dusted sweatpants, pouring love into a pot of spaghetti, setting the table with mismatched dishes and laughter. She was present. She was enough.

The more I let go of the expectations I'd placed on myself, the more space I found to live fully in the life I actually had, not the one I felt like I was failing at.

Letting go of the cookbooks wasn't the death of a dream. It was the beginning of a better one with freedom from the performance and with permission to be the kind of woman who creates joy without needing it to look a certain way.

When the Dream Still Matters—Just Not Like Before

The running shoes, however, were different from the cookbooks. They carried a dream I still held on to: running a marathon. When I walked through the three questions with those shoes, I saw the nuance.

- **Story:** The shoes symbolized strength and follow-through. I could picture myself crossing a finish line and proving to myself that I could do hard things.

- **Season:** That dream didn't match my current season. I had two kids under two and no time to sleep, let alone train. It didn't mean the dream was wrong for me; it just wasn't for right now.
- **Self:** I asked, "Do I still want this?" The answer was yes, but not the all-or-nothing version. Maybe I didn't need to run 26.2 miles to prove something. Maybe a 5K would feel just as powerful.

So I kept the shoes but shifted their purpose. They weren't a reminder of what I *hadn't* done. They became an inspiring sign of what I could still accomplish as I redefined what success with them could look like.

Letting go doesn't always mean saying goodbye. Sometimes it just means rewriting the story.

What If It's All of the Above?

As we close out the discussion of the four clutter types (superficial, scarcity, sentimental, and identity), I want to leave you with one last truth: Not everything fits neatly into a single box.

That blender you never use? It might be scarcity clutter ("I spent good money on this"), aspirational clutter ("I was going to be a smoothie person"), and guilt clutter all rolled into one.

That heirloom teacup from your grandmother? Maybe it's sentimental—and something you keep because you feel like you should.

The point isn't to label every item perfectly. The point is to understand why you're holding on so you can reach for the right tool to let go.

Now that you've unpacked the beliefs and motivations behind each clutter type, maybe you've begun to soften the fear and approach decision-making with trust and honesty instead of insecurity or shame. The next time you find yourself standing in front of that drawer or closet or storage bin, unsure of what's keeping you stuck, you'll know how to start.

And when you do, you won't only be decluttering. You'll be coming home to yourself.

REFLECT

Think about the items in your home that are most tied to intense emotions. How is holding on to these items affecting your mental and emotional space? Are these items inspiring you or weighing you down?

TAKE ACTION

Choose one item you suspect might fall into the category of identity clutter. Then use the Story, Season, Self questions to evaluate it with clarity and compassion.

- **Story:** What story have I tied to this item? Is this my story, or someone else's? Do I want to keep living this version of myself, or is it time to write a new chapter? (Give yourself permission to consider if the item is part of a narrative you've outgrown.)
- **Season:** Is this item relevant to the season of life I'm in now? Does this fit my current time, energy, and responsibilities? (Just because something mattered once doesn't mean it belongs in your life today.) Am I holding on out of hope, guilt, or nostalgia for a season I've already moved on from?
- **Self:** Does this align with who I am now—or who I truly want to become? Does this feel like an invitation—or an obligation? Am I clinging to an old ideal or creating space for a truer, freer version of me? (Let go of items tied to who you thought you needed to be. Keep what supports who you are becoming.)

If you decide to keep it, place it intentionally in a spot where it supports you. If you decide to let it go, release it knowing you're making space for the life you truly want.

Repeat this process with another item when you feel ready, taking small, confident steps toward clarity and alignment in your home.

These three questions won't just help you clear physical space. They'll help you release the pressure to become someone you're not—so you can fully step into who you already are.

Chapter 8

How to Get and Stay Motivated

I was in seventh grade when I joined the track team for the first time. I'd never raced competitively before, but there was something about sprinting that felt electrifying to me. The sound of the starting gun going off, the explosive push off the blocks, and the rush of adrenaline as your body surges forward. I loved short sprints—the 100-meter, the 200. Those first few strides are pure freedom. Your muscles stretch, your heart races, the wind rushes past—and for a few seconds, it feels like nothing can stop you.

But then came the 400-meter dash. A full lap around the track felt like punishment to me. Holding that speed for an entire quarter mile? I hated it. The burn came fast, and I'd run out of steam before I even hit the final stretch.

My coach would always say the same thing: "The key to the 400 is pacing. Go out too fast, and you'll burn out. Run smart, and you'll finish strong." At the time, I rolled my eyes. Pace myself? Why would I hold back when I could blast through it like my 100-meter sprints?

But after a few painful, gasping (losing) finishes, I learned: The 400 wasn't about speed. It was about strategy. About having enough energy to carry you all the way through.

The shift happened when I stopped trying to win the race in the first 100 meters. I held back. I stuck to the plan. And when I hit the final turn, I had the strength to finish strong.

That's when I realized: This wasn't just about running. It was about clarity. Because when you're clear on the goal—and how to get there—you don't put energy into the wrong pace. You stay grounded, focused, and calm. You don't sprint yourself into burnout. You move with intention.

It turns out that lesson shows up everywhere.

I did the same thing in my home as an adult. One weekend I'd decided to finally declutter our garage. I was fired up. I had watched the videos, saved the checklists, and committed to "doing it the right way." Step one? Pull everything out. So I did. Bikes. Boxes. Baby gear we hadn't touched in years. Half-used paint cans. It all came out on to the driveway like I was starring in my own home makeover show.

I stood in the driveway, sweat dripping down my back, holding a half-eaten granola bar in one hand and a dusty tote lid in the other. The kids were fighting over sidewalk chalk. My phone buzzed with a work email. And all I could think was: *What am I even doing?* This wasn't peace—it was a circus.

What the method didn't account for was this: real life.

About twenty minutes in, the kids needed lunch. Then someone had a meltdown. Then I realized I hadn't carved out nearly enough time to finish. So I shoved half the stuff back in "just for now." Except "just for now" turned into three weeks. Then three months.

Every time I walked by that garage, I felt the same tightness in my chest. The project wasn't only unfinished—it was now bigger, messier, and heavier. The guilt piled up like the clutter did.

And that's when I realized: I hadn't failed; I just didn't have clarity. It was like trying to run a 400-meter dash without a plan. Once I got clear on my goals and my approach—why I was doing this, what I wanted out of it, and how I wanted *to feel* in my home—everything changed.

I didn't need to rush. I needed to pace myself. I didn't need to do it all. I needed to focus on what mattered. Gaining clarity gave me permission to zoom out and stop reacting. Instead, I started leading.

At this point in the book, you've learned about your Stuff Story, the Good Enough Home philosophy, and the four types of clutter. I hope you feel like the lights have turned on (you know more of what you're in the middle of) and there's a sense of freedom in the air (you know you get to decide what your goals are).

From here you might have some bursts of motivation and moments of big progress. And then times of feeling overwhelmed, exhausted, or directionless might follow. What do you do when you feel like you've run out of steam? How do you "run smart" in this journey of home transformation?

You need more clarity—about what will make your home your happy place, why you'll do the work of creating it, and what small steps you can keep taking toward it.

This is where the Clarity Compass comes in. It's a simple, three-step process to help you get clear on what you want, why you want it, and how to make consistent, sustainable progress without burning out.

Let's sharpen your view of the goal ahead and find your pace for moving toward it.

Step 1: Name Your Big Why

You don't need a Big Why when the playlist is pumping, the sun is shining, and you've got energy to spare. You need it when your legs feel like lead, you're gasping for air, and a long, daunting path stretches out ahead of you.

The equivalent of this at home could be when you're standing in the hallway, exhausted, staring at another mess you didn't make. When the progress feels invisible and decluttering feels pointless. When you're tempted to shove everything back in the drawer and walk away.

Will there be days you don't want to do this work? Days when your energy is gone, when life feels too loud, when the couch is calling and the clutter feels endless? Of course. That's the reason you need a Big Why to keep you motivated and focused. It's your anchor in the storm. Your compass when you feel lost.

Let's go back to the basics of your current reality. Clutter is stealing something from you—your time, your peace, your energy. It's keeping you stuck in a cycle of trying to catch up and being distracted from living fully. You want that to change, and it can.

You'll start to make it happen by naming *exactly* what you want back.

Research out of UCLA's Center on Everyday Lives and Families (CELF) found that women who describe their homes as cluttered exhibit chronically elevated cortisol levels—the stress hormone linked to fatigue, anxiety, and inflammation—even when their daily routines are comparable to those in less cluttered homes.[1] In other words, more clutter equals more stress. It is not imagined or exaggerated; it's real. And over time, that chronic, low-grade stress takes a toll emotionally, mentally, and physically.

Are you feeling seen yet?

Identifying how this is happening for you will inform your Big Why. Soon I'll guide you with some questions to do that, but first I want you to see a few examples of a Big Why. Here are some from my students:

- "I want to sit on the couch at night and actually rest, not feel like I should be folding laundry."
- "I want a home that feels like a sanctuary, where I can finally exhale and reconnect with God."

- "I want to feel like myself again. I want to laugh more, play with my kids, and actually feel happy in my own home."
- "I want my daughter to remember a joyful home, not a stressed-out mom who never sat down to play."

A Big Why has to be big enough to pull you forward when motivation fades, hitting you deep enough to remind you why this work matters. It needs to fuel you forward while also steering you toward results that empower you.

Knowing your Big Why helps shrink the overwhelm. Every drawer you tackle, every item you release is not just progress; it's power. You get a taste of what change is like—how reclaiming your peace, control, and energy feels.

To uncover your Big Why, start reflecting on these guiding questions:

1. **What's the hardest part of living in my home right now?** Is it the mess that resets faster than you can manage it? The never-ending laundry cycle? The pit in your stomach when someone drops by and you panic about them seeing your space? Is it the arguments with your partner about who is doing more? The resentment that simmers beneath the surface because it always seems to fall on you?
2. **What would feel possible if my home weren't a source of stress?** Would mornings start with connection instead of chaos? Would you stop snapping at your kids—not because they changed, but because you finally have margin? Would you stop canceling plans

or apologizing for the state of your house? Would you walk through your front door and exhale instead of brace? Would you finally see yourself again—beyond the mess, the mental load, the to-do list?

3. **What is clutter costing me?** Are you wasting time hunting for things you know you own? Spending money replacing what's buried under piles? Feeling mentally fried from the constant background noise of visual chaos? Or maybe it's deeper. Has clutter become a silent thief of joy, presence, intimacy, and self-worth? Is it driving a wedge into your relationships—or your relationship with *yourself*?

These questions will probably bring a lot to the surface for you to consider. Once you can see the many factors at play, ask:

- Which reason hits the hardest?
- Which one, if changed, would give me the biggest breath of relief?
- What is the result that could come from decluttering that I'm craving most?

It might be finally having a rhythm with your partner where the mental load isn't all on you. It might be walking into your home after a long workday and feeling your nervous system relax instead of spike. It might be having the confidence to invite friends over without scrambling to clean—or apologizing for the mess.

Your Big Why doesn't have to be poetic, but it should

be personal. It should make you feel something in your gut and maybe even bring a tear to your eye. It's a vision of what your unique "happy place" home would look and feel like. It's a declaration about what you're choosing for yourself.

Write down your Big Why. Say it out loud. Stick it to your fridge. It's what will carry you through the hard days, the hidden piles, and the "I don't have time" spiral. It's what will remind you—this isn't just about your stuff; it's about your life. You're building something that truly feels like home.

Step 2: Define Each Space with Intention

Now that you've named what matters most, it's time to bring that vision to life—one space at a time. How do you want each room to function? How do you want it to feel? That's what step 2 is all about. Maybe your bedroom doesn't feel calm; instead, it's loaded with unfolded laundry and half-finished projects. Or maybe your home office doesn't inspire focus because piles of unopened mail, school art, and rogue cords always greet you when you walk in.

You're building something that truly feels like home.

Spaces that aren't supporting you usually are also draining you. As author Joshua Becker puts it, "Our possessions either help us fulfill our purpose, or they distract us from it."[2] When a space is misaligned with your vision, it doesn't just frustrate; it drags you down. And that frustration doesn't stay in the room. It affects your energy, your mood, and even your relationships. You're not only missing the support you need from each room but also managing clutter—and friction.

You start to change that by giving each room a job, a role, a reason to exist. When you define what a space is for—and who it's for—it becomes easier to see what no longer fits.

It's a little like plugging a destination into a navigation app. Without a clear direction, clutter takes the wheel. But when you define the function, the users, and the feeling you want in each space, you'll be in control, designing it the way you want.

Here's a Space Intention Check you can work through before you declutter. Keep in mind these questions aren't about where things stand now but about where you're headed.

- What do I want this space to be for?
- Whom do I want it to serve—and how?
- How do I want to feel when I'm in it?

Let's walk through a few real-world examples to help you imagine how it could look for you.

Bedroom

- **Purpose:** A space for rest and reconnection.
- **Used by:** You and your partner.
- **I want to feel:** Soft. Calm. Restful.

Kitchen

- **Purpose:** A place to prep food and gather around meals.
- **Used by:** The whole family, multiple times a day.
- **I want to feel:** Warm. Efficient. Grounded.

Living Room

- **Purpose:** A space to relax, connect, and spend time together.
- **Used by:** Everyone—including guests.
- **I want to feel:** Invited. Settled. Together.

When you walk into a room that's aligned with its purpose, the people who use it, and how you want to feel, you'll have the power of clarity. It'll make your decluttering decisions so much easier.

Step 3: Set Boundaries to Protect Your Space

Once you've defined the purpose of your spaces, the next step is to protect that purpose with boundaries. Your clarity won't last without them. We discussed boundaries in chapter 4 in the Five Basic Steps of Decluttering, but because they're so critical, we'll look at them again now in the Clarity Compass.

Maybe you have a drawer in your home that barely closes. It started out innocent enough. Just your basic kitchen utensils. Then came the melon baller you've used once, extra spatulas, and that avocado slicer you were convinced would change your life. Now every time you open it, it sighs under the weight. And so do you.

That drawer is what life without boundaries looks like.

Boundaries keep your home aligned with your Big Why, even when life gets busy. They cut down on decision fatigue, making it easier for you to see when something's no longer serving you. They give you a built-in goal, a finish line—so you're not decluttering forever.

Here are a few quick examples of how setting boundaries can play out.

Joanna knew her overflowing book collection was quietly weighing her down. She had books stacked on the floor, in baskets, even under her bed. So she gave herself a clear container: one bookshelf. No more. She went from three overflowing shelves to one intentional collection. Now when she walks by it, she doesn't feel overwhelmed; she feels grounded.

Sally's closet had become a source of daily frustration. It was stuffed to the brim. Clothes were spilling on to her bedroom floor. We started with one goal: make everything fit comfortably inside her closet. Then, we used the bins she already owned to create boundaries within the space: one for undergarments, one for tanks, one for sleepwear. No more overflowing drawers. No more guessing what belonged where. The closet became easier to maintain because every category had a clear home with clear limits.

Kelly felt like she was constantly picking up toys—and never seeing a difference. She realized her kids had no clear limits. So she started by defining one: a single closet. If the toys didn't fit, something had to go. Suddenly, cleanup became doable. Even better? Her kids started helping—because the system finally made sense.

These women created personalized solutions that fit their lives, their spaces, and their goals. What they set up didn't have to look like anyone else's home or be impressive enough for social media posts. Boundaries don't have to be fancy or cover a big space. They can be a room, a drawer, a shelf, or even a single bin. What matters isn't the size or aesthetic—it's that they work.

Boundaries act like reset buttons. They give you both a finish line to aim for and a safety net that keeps clutter from creeping back in. When things start to spill over, your boundaries do what they're designed to do: They signal it's time to pause and reassess. You're not starting from scratch. You're adjusting, realigning, and continuing with confidence.

Boundaries make the difference between random tidying and intentional maintenance. When you pair them with your Big Why and a clear purpose for your space, they become the final piece of your Clarity Compass.

Common Challenges and Missteps

When you first establish your Clarity Compass, you might get so motivated that you start thinking big—*Time for an overhaul!* It's easy to assume that's the answer and jump to it right away, but I'll offer a word of caution about that. I've learned from working with thousands of women that what we first *think we need* is often not what ends up *actually working*. It's also usually the equivalent of biting off more than we can chew, which only sets us up for overwhelm.

For instance, we think we need more bins. Or a better schedule. We think if we could just "get caught up," everything else would fall into place.

But the reality is, most of us aren't "behind"—we're buried. The problem feels extreme, so we assume the solution must be as well. We don't realize we've been managing our homes *reactively* instead of intentionally, so slowing down and approaching a space with an entirely new mindset really does become a game-changer.

When you name what matters, you stop doing what doesn't. And then a few key, effective shifts will make all the difference—no overhaul needed.

This especially applies to spaces that hold multiple purposes. Say you work from your kitchen table, or sometimes your roommate treats the living room like an art studio. That's fine; it's real life. But without clarity, those shared, overlapping spaces will stop serving you and start swallowing you whole.

A perfect example of this is my kitchen. I used to joke that it was the heart of our home—until it started giving me heart palpitations. It wasn't the cooking or the kids underfoot; it was everything else. I'd walk in to make dinner and instantly feel my chest tighten. There'd be papers piled on the counters. Crayons on the floor. A sock near the fridge (still no idea how it got there).

Over time, the kitchen had quietly become everything:

meal station. Homework zone. Mail-sorting desk. Emotional dump site. And the more it absorbed, the more overwhelmed I felt.

I thought I needed to try harder. Get more baskets. Make a better chore chart. Organize the junk drawer once and for all. But none of those things ultimately proved helpful long-term.

That's when I turned to my Clarity Compass.

Step 1: I named my Big Why.

I couldn't cook dinner efficiently without shifting science projects or sorting mail first. I wanted an open space to put all the dinner-prep items and not have to scramble to clear the chaos at mealtime. I didn't need a Pinterest kitchen. I needed peace.

Step 2: I defined the space with intention.

I paused to ask the right questions: How do I need this kitchen to function? Who is using it—and how? How do I want to feel when I'm here?

This wasn't just about labeling the room "kitchen"; it was about designing it to serve our real life. I needed a place to prep meals, connect over dinner, help with homework, and still feel grounded in the middle of all that. The space had to work for the whole family multiple times a day—without making me feel like I was constantly cleaning up after a tornado.

I wanted it to feel warm, efficient, and supportive.

Step 3: I set boundaries.

This is where the transformation really started to take root through the small, intentional lines I drew.

The homework supplies used to scatter across the table, so I cleared out the back half of our silverware drawer and turned it into their new home. I made it neatly organized, easy to access, easy to reset.

There had been a mountain of school papers that once lived (and died) on the kitchen counter. So I added a labeled bin by the shoe bench, right where the backpacks always landed. Now those papers had a smart, limited place to live without taking over the kitchen.

There also had been an endless pile of "just-in-case" gadgets. I made a new rule that if any of them didn't get used weekly, they wouldn't live on the counter. The waffle maker found a new home in the pantry. The old toaster went in the donation pile.

These solutions worked for us. Every time something started to spill over again, those boundaries gave me a built-in check-in—not a moment of panic, but a moment to reassess.

Turning Clarity into Action: Your Path Forward

When you gain clarity about what matters most, everything else gets easier. You start making decisions with intention and strength. You create open space around you, which also frees up space in your mind, your mood, your moments. Clarity gives that space back.

And the more you take action with focused clarity—one drawer, one boundary, one reset at a time—the more likely you'll do it in other places in your life. How you spend your time, how you show up for your people, even how you feel in your own skin. You'll be in the practice of living grounded, of being intentional.

Your clarity is going to give all your decision-making moments a North Star, even as your home—like your life—is constantly evolving. The spaces you live in should grow and shift alongside your changing needs, routines, and priorities. You can use the Clarity Compass to create a path forward whenever life changes. You also can use it as an anchor when things feel off course.

The spaces you live in should grow and shift alongside your changing needs, routines, and priorities.

At this moment in the journey, though, I hope you hold on to this: You're allowed to redefine what a space is for. You're allowed to pivot. You're allowed to make it simpler. That's not failure, that's growth.

You don't need to fix everything this week. You just need to start. One choice. One corner. One small win. That's where momentum lives—not in the overwhelm of everything, but in the courage to begin.

In the next chapter, we'll

look at some sustainable systems that can turn your clarity into consistent, life-giving action. You've already started something powerful, and I'm going to help you keep moving forward.

REFLECT

Start giving some thought to your Big Why. What is the biggest pain point of your experience in your home right now? What struggle, friction, or longing are you feeling most frequently and intensely? If I told you that you could build a path to any improved version of your living space, try to envision what that improved version would look like and feel like.

Now try articulating this in a simple sentence. For example, "I want to sit on the couch at night and actually rest, not feel like I should be folding laundry."

Revisit and revise this as much as you need to.

Once you settle on why your decluttering work is worth the effort, you'll be able to stay fueled on the path ahead.

TAKE ACTION

Pick one small area of your home that is stressing you out instead of supporting you. Work through the three Clarity Compass questions to evaluate how to handle the clutter, imagine ways to improve the space, and set it up for success.

- **Why do I need a change here?** Name your Big Why, the new experience in that space that matters to you.
- **What do I want from this space?** Define its purpose, who will use it, and the feeling you want to have in it.
- **How could I keep it from backsliding?** Set boundaries so the space can keep supporting you.

Chapter 9

Systems That Do the Heavy Lifting

Some seasons of life feel like one long game of catch-up. You're constantly reacting, constantly adjusting. You tell yourself it'll slow down soon, but the finish line keeps moving. I know that feeling well.

For years, I kept thinking that if I just tried a little harder, I could stay on top of it all. But the truth is, effort wasn't the problem. I didn't need to hustle harder; I needed to stop relying on memory, willpower, and last-minute scrambles to run my home. What I really needed was a system.

Every Sunday night, I promised myself this would be *the week*. The week I stayed ahead of the laundry. The week mornings ran smoother. The week I didn't feel like I was juggling fire by Thursday. But by Wednesday, I was back in survival mode—again.

Maybe you've had weeks like that too—the kind where

you feel like your home is running you, instead of the other way around.

Do I need more motivation? I wondered. *More discipline? More coffee?*

Nope.

It took a while, but over time, I realized I had a system problem.

By the term *system*, I mean a repeatable process or structure that simplifies how something gets done. When you hear the word *systems*, do you picture restraints and burdens? Order and direction? For some, systems sound helpful; for others, they sound like one more thing to manage. As an expert on habits, James Clear has a compelling view: "You do not rise to the level of your goals," he wrote. "You fall to the level of your systems."[1]

Systems are the invisible scaffolding that hold up your home life. They answer the daily "what now?" before it has a chance to stress you out. Without a system, we default to decision fatigue. Clutter builds. Mental load doubles. And we keep wondering why we feel behind, when we're really just missing the invisible support.

A good system doesn't ask more from you; it gives back. It catches the dropped balls. Automates the mundane. Eases the mental load you've been carrying solo. If you've ever said, "I just need to get more organized," what you might actually need is a better system.

In this chapter, I'm going to show you how to build one—step-by-step—with flexibility, clarity, and the grace to shift as your life does.

The DASH Framework: Systems That Stick

You don't need a system for everything. But if there's one area in your home that feels like it's constantly falling apart—where routines unravel and stress runs high—it probably needs one.

The tool I'll share in this chapter is a home management framework called DASH, which stands for Declutter, Assess, Systematize, and Habitualize. Whether it's laundry piles, paper clutter, or after-school chaos, DASH gives you a simple way to bring order, flow, and function to your most frustrating spaces.

I created this method for myself and for the women I coach when "just get organized" wasn't cutting it anymore. I use it all the time now. When something in my home isn't working, I go back to it; it's that essential. And especially as life changes and seasons shift, DASH helps my home adjust too.

Here's the breakdown:

1. **Declutter:** Clear out the excess that's making everything harder.
2. **Assess:** Pinpoint the real issue (not just the mess you see).
3. **Systemize:** Create a structure that supports your real life.
4. **Habitualize:** Build small, repeatable actions that make it stick.

It's not just a checklist. It's a clarity tool. This is how you can zoom out, cut through the noise, and build a home that works for you.

DASH in Action: Rachel's Story

Every time Rachel walked through the door of her home, she felt like chaos greeted her. Shoes were scattered like breadcrumbs. Unopened mail layered like sediment. Shopping bags from last week (or maybe last month) leaned against the stairs, waiting for someone to remember them.

Rachel didn't need more bins or labels or even a massive purge. She needed a system that could hold her life.

Step 1: Declutter—Clear the Friction

Before you can create a system, you need to remove what's getting in the way of it. This step isn't just about tossing items; it's about clearing friction so you can see what's left to work with.

Rachel's entryway wasn't packed to the ceiling; it didn't scream *chaos*. But the subtle layers of excess had built up, enough to slow everything down and make walking through the door feel like trudging through knee-high mud.

We started not by talking about systems or habits but by stepping into the space and looking at it with fresh eyes. Here's what we noticed:

- more shoes than her entryway could hold (even the "daily" pairs were spilling out and tripping her up);
- mail that no longer mattered (expired coupons, junk ads, bills that had already been paid);

- shopping bags from weeks ago, still waiting to be returned (now just visual noise);
- coats (when it was summertime, so they were misplaced).

It was all "just too much." And when your home is doing too much, you end up carrying the extra weight.

Next, we removed superficial clutter, using our definition of *clutter* as our North Star: anything that isn't actively supporting her life right now. Any broken, unused, or duplicate items left the area.

Then, I walked Rachel through these questions:

- What's creating the most friction right now? Where do you feel stuck the moment you step into this space?
- Is there any scarcity, sentimental, or identity clutter to remove?

These questions were about helping Rachel see the space clearly, without guilt or guesswork.

From there, the progress was fast:

- Three pairs of shoes she never wore, aspirational identity clutter, gone.
- A pile of junk mail shredded and recycled.
- A backpack no one had touched in six months, scarcity clutter, donated.
- Two coats she no longer reached for, out the door.

- A handful of "this doesn't belong here" items, returned to their actual homes.

Each small decision removed a piece of the noise. After a while Rachel stood back and said something I hear all the time: "It's like I can finally breathe in here."

That's what decluttering does. It doesn't just create space—it creates relief. It gives your next step a solid place to land. And in many cases, that might be enough.

If Rachel already had systems and habits in place to support the flow of that space, she probably would've been good to go. Sometimes all a room needs is a reset—a quick round of decluttering to get things back on track. But Rachel wanted to make sure the space would stay that way. She wanted maintenance, not just momentum. That's where the next step came in.

Step 2: Assess—Find the Root of the Issue

Here we pause and ask deeper questions:

- What's the true purpose of this space?
- What's still not flowing?
- What patterns keep repeating despite the clutter being gone?

When Rachel took a closer look, two things stood out: the shoes and the returns.

Even with fewer shoes, the bench still overflowed. Not because there were "too many," but because they weren't being put away consistently. Without a system in place, even a small pile-up created that nagging sense of disorder all over again.

Then came the returns. Shopping bags were still ending up on the floor, the stairs, the console—wherever they landed in the moment. Rachel wasn't forgetting them because she didn't care; she just didn't have a clear, repeatable place to put them.

This is what assessing helps us do: It shines a light on what's still making the space feel hard so we can remove that friction at the source.

Rachel's *aha* moment came quickly: "I don't need more baskets," she realized. "I just need this space to make sense with how I live."

So she made two quick decisions:

- Limit the entryway to three pairs of shoes each for her and her husband.
- Add a return hook by the door, so shopping returns in limbo had a home.

With those tiny shifts, the space didn't only look better—it started to work better.

Step 3: Systemize—Make It Easier to Succeed

Rachel had cleared the clutter, clarified her boundaries, and uncovered what wasn't working. Now she needed a repeatable way for things to run smoothly—especially around shoes and returns, the two biggest friction points in her entryway.

How could we keep the entryway maintained with the least amount of energy?

We talked about her shoes first. Since she'd limited the space to three pairs per person, we brainstormed how to keep it tidy:

- A daily thirty-second reset before bed?
- A quick check-in once a week during her Sunday routine?

Here's where a lot of people overthink trying to find the "perfect" system, assuming there must be only one right path forward. But you don't need perfection here; you need consistency.

So, looking at our two brainstorms, I asked her, "Which one feels more doable for you?"

Rachel knew herself. "If I let it build up, I'll avoid it," she said. "A quick reset each night feels easier."

Done.

Next, we looked at returns. The hook was in place, but now she needed a rhythm to go with it.

Again, we kept it simple:

- Add returns to her weekly errand list?
- Or check the hook daily and grab one on the way out?

She chose the weekly errand approach because it already existed in her routine. That meant she didn't have to create a new habit—she'd just attach a tiny action to something she was already doing.

This is what systemizing looks like in real life: small tweaks anchored to your actual rhythms, designed to remove friction, not add more to your to-do list.

Rachel wasn't aiming for a Pinterest-worthy entryway. She was building a process that would stick—without burning her out.

That's the power of having a system that fits you.

Step 4: Habitualize—The Glue That Holds It All Together

Systems set the stage, but habits keep the story going.

This final step isn't about doing more. It's about making less feel like enough—on autopilot. Rachel had decluttered. She had systems in place. Now, she needed rhythms that helped her follow through without having to think about it every time.

We kept it simple. Instead of dropping her shoes "just for now," she decided in the moment—rack or closet. This approach followed the OHIO rule: *Only Handle It Once*. This popular acronym has been used by professional organizers for decades to encourage quicker, more intentional decisions.

She did the same thing with returns: no more bags drifting around the entryway. She placed them on the hook right away. One touch. Done.

Then came her evening reset. It wasn't a chore or a checklist. Just thirty seconds to scan the space after dinner—toss a flyer, straighten the shoes, glance at the hook. Enough to keep the chaos from creeping back in.

Rachel didn't reinvent herself to maintain her space. She simply stacked one small habit on to a system that already worked. And over time, those tiny, almost forgettable decisions added up to something powerful: peace, predictability, and a sense of control in a space that used to overwhelm her.

The system will guide you in consistency, and consistency will create support. So, even on the off days (because, of course, there will be off days), you won't be starting from scratch. You'll simply be stepping back into a flow you've already built.

This is what DASH was made for. Not to give you more to do, but to give you a way back to ease, even when life is full.

The Power of Evolving Systems

One year after Rachel first used DASH to rescue her entryway from constant chaos, life looked very different for her. Within the span of a year, she became a mom to twins. What had once been a simple system for two adults now had to stretch to fit the unpredictable, high-gear rhythm of family life.

The entryway—her old pain point turned peaceful pass-through—had become a pain point again, this time with diaper bags, tiny shoes, and a stroller that never seemed to land in the same place twice.

But instead of spiraling or assuming she'd "failed,"

Rachel did what she'd learned to do: She returned to what she knew. She opened her DASH toolbox and got to work.

She started with *Declutter*.

Extra shoes, off-season coats, random items that had slowly crept back in—she cleared them all.

She asked: "Is this actively supporting our life right now?"

For the noes, she added them to her donation pile.

For the yeses, she moved them into *Assess*—looking at what was left and how it was functioning (or not).

She wasn't just creating physical space. She was creating capacity—for smoother mornings, less scrambling, and more calm at the door.

Then came the *Assess* step.

Rachel looked at what was left—the yes items. The diaper bags were being used daily. The stroller made every outing possible. The baby gear was key for this season.

All these items were essentials, but did they all need to live in the entryway? That small space had become the catch-all for everything, and it simply couldn't keep up.

Instead of trying to force everything to fit, she looked at her home as a whole. What else was nearby? What space could take on some of the load?

That's when Rachel implemented a secondary drop zone inside the garage. It wasn't fancy, just a small shelving unit, a hook for diaper bags, and a corner for the stroller to live—folded, out of the way, but easy to grab. Suddenly, her entryway didn't have to carry the full weight of daily life.

Then came the *Systematize* step.

With the clutter cleared and the true pain points

identified, Rachel was ready to rebuild. Not from scratch, but from a place of clarity.

With the stroller and diaper bags now living in a secondary drop zone in the garage, the entryway had room to breathe. Rachel took a step back and asked herself, *What needs to happen in this space?*

Here's what she landed on:

- Her twins needed a place to stash their tiny shoes—somewhere low, open, and easy.
- She needed a home for grab-and-go items like wipes, snacks, and sunglasses.
- She needed a catch-all for the random stuff that always managed to appear—hair ties, receipts, small toys.

So she created a simple system:

- a low bin for shoes right by the door
- a small basket inside the closet for essentials
- one catch-all container for stray items, which she planned to empty every Sunday night

And finally, the *Habitualize* step.

Rachel brought back her evening reset. After the twins were in bed and the house quieted down, she gave the entryway sixty seconds of love. Shoes got tossed into the bin. The stroller spot in the garage got a quick glance. The catch-all container got scanned and, if she had the energy, tidied.

She wasn't always consistent. Some nights, she skipped it. But most nights, it happened. Because she had made it easy.

Rachel also kept using the OHIO rule—*Only Handle It Once*. If she walked in with baby snacks, sunglasses, or a shopping receipt, she didn't drop them and promise to deal with them later. She put them away right then. Even if she wasn't consistent 100 percent of the time, she was consistent enough to make a difference.

That's the power of a habit built around who you are and what life looks like right now—not who you wish you were or what someone else on the internet is doing.

You don't need to overhaul your whole home to feel at ease.

And the result? Rachel didn't just have a tidy entryway. She had peace. She had predictability.

You don't need to overhaul your whole home to feel at ease. You just need one system that gives more than it takes. That's the power of DASH—it meets you where you are, works with the season you're in, and evolves with you as life changes. Start with one space. One routine. One repeatable win. Because when systems support your life, life feels lighter.

REFLECT

Think of areas in your home that are a source of frustration. It could be they're missing a system—something simple and repeatable that supports your life. Use the following questions to help you uncover where you might need a system and can start using DASH to make a real, lasting change.

- **Declutter:** Is it clutter, a lack of organization, or simply a space that never stays tidy no matter how often you clean it?
- **Assess:** How might clutter be adding friction to that frustration? Are there items you don't use, things that don't belong, or objects with no clear home?
- **Systematize:** Are there systems or habits that could reduce the chaos? Would a reset help maintain order? Would decluttering lighten the load? Does the space need clearer zones or storage solutions?
- **Habitualize:** What's one small habit you could anchor to this space—a quick reset, a two-minute tidy, or a rule like OHIO—that would make it easier to maintain?

If something feels overwhelming, it may not be because you "aren't doing enough"; it may mean the system isn't fully in place yet.

TAKE ACTION

Choose one area of your home to focus on this week using DASH. The goal isn't to fix everything at once but to build a system that works.

- **Declutter:** Start by removing the excess. Clear out what's no longer serving you so you can see the real friction points underneath. This is where most people stop, but it's only step one.

- **Assess:** Once the clutter is out of the way, ask yourself, *What's still not working here? What keeps breaking down?* Look for the root issue—not only the mess, but the function. The flow. The pinch points.
- **Systemize:** Now you're ready to create a structure that supports your real life. Not an ideal version of it. Choose something simple and repeatable that fits your current season. Don't overcomplicate it—start small and build from there.
- **Habitualize:** This is where the magic happens. Layer in tiny habits that help the system run without you having to think about it. You don't have to do it 100 percent consistently, just consistently enough. It could be a thirty-second reset at night or putting something away right when you walk in the door.

DASH isn't about doing more. It's about building systems that do the heavy lifting for you. The more you use DASH, the more natural it will become. You'll spot where friction is building, know what questions to ask, and trust yourself to tweak things when life shifts.

Chapter 10

Onboarding the Adults in Your Home

Sometimes the hardest part of sharing a space with another adult isn't the big stuff—it's the tiny, silent negotiations that play out day after day. One person sees a task and takes care of it right away. The other doesn't even notice it. You're both living in the same space but experiencing it in completely different ways. You're not asking for perfection; you just desperately want to feel like the responsibility of caring and keeping things running isn't always landing on you. And then, it happens again.

You walk into the kitchen—*deep sigh*. A coffee mug on the counter, half full. Shoes kicked off in the walkway, just waiting to be tripped over. Today's mail scattered across the counter (even though you cleared it off this morning). A jacket draped over a dining chair you've asked them not to use as a closet. It's not a crisis, but it chips away at you.

If you don't say anything, it'll stay exactly like this—for hours, maybe days. Until you're the one who moves it.

After all the effort you've poured into simplifying, organizing, and creating systems, you're the one holding the line and asking yourself familiar questions. *Do I pick it all up myself—again? Do I remind them—again? Do I ask them to get rid of their junk—again?* Deep down, you already know how this plays out.

The most frustrating part isn't just the stuff. It's the constant gnawing thought, *Why am I the only one who seems to care?*

If you've tried to lead by example, dropped hints, drawn lines, or even lost your cool a few times, you're not alone. I've been there too. But at one point, things changed: I stopped trying to convince my husband to care. Instead I focused my energy in a few other directions: I worked on an area I knew I could help influence him—our environment. I approached conversations with him about stuff in an undemanding, unaggressive way. And I reframed how I viewed some of our spaces. Over time, these shifts proved effective.

Whether you live with a partner, roommate, or another adult, this chapter will help you find a way forward as you manage your living space with them—even if they're not fully on board. Not through blaming or louder conversations, but through far more subtle—and surprisingly powerful—approaches.

Design Your Space for Follow-Through

We tend to believe that change starts with a big talk or a perfectly explained request. But in reality, behavior shifts don't need to begin with a conversation. They can begin with the environment.

James Clear said it best: "Environment is the invisible hand that shapes human behavior."[1] That means your surroundings aren't just background; they're behavioral triggers. Whether we realize it or not, the layout of our homes is constantly influencing what we do or don't do. So when clutter builds or tasks are skipped, the cause isn't necessarily resistance; there might just be invisible friction in the environment.

Remember, our brains are biologically wired to conserve energy. Every time we're faced with a decision, even something as small as *Where does this go?* or *Should I deal with this now or later?* it uses mental energy. And the more effort something requires, the more likely the brain is to punt it for "later." So when your partner or roommate drops their bag on the floor and walks away, it's not (always) because they're careless. It's that the alternative, putting it away, might not be the easiest option.

We've all been there: A family member says they'll put things away, but somehow the stuff still ends up scattered, piled, or dropped in the usual spots. It's tempting to think, *Why can't they just follow through?* But often the issue isn't laziness; it's friction. The environment is working against the behavior you're hoping to see.

When we reduce the number of steps it takes to do something, though, we increase the chances it gets done right the first time.

That's why I always come back to Design for Follow-Through—an approach that shifts the focus from trying to "fix" the person to shaping the space. You're not forcing participation. You're removing the barriers that make participation harder than it needs to be and designing the space to help them succeed.

Let's look at how friction hides in plain sight.

- Keys landing on the counter instead of in the tray—because the tray is tucked in a drawer across the room.
  → Try placing the tray where keys naturally get dropped, even if it's not your ideal aesthetic spot.
- Shoes scattered near the door—because the storage is upstairs and no one wants to climb the stairs to put them away.
  → Add a basket, low shelf, or shoe mat right by the actual entry point—even if it's just temporary overflow.
- Mail piling on the island—because the inbox is out of sight.
  → Bring the inbox into the visual flow. Put a small vertical sorter or tray on the counter until a habit of sorting mail is formed. (Later, consider putting the sorter or tray near the counter, where it's still visible but less prominent.)
- Gym bags lingering in the hallway—because there's no hook or shelf where people typically drop them.
  → Install a hook or bin right by the drop zone, not where you wish they'd drop it, but where they already do. (Again, you can try changing the spot later; first, make it easy for them to learn to put gym bags where they live.)

The easier it is to complete the action in the moment, the more likely it is to happen.

Now, does this mean your living room floor needs to become the new designated spot for shoe storage? Of course not. You're allowed to want a beautiful, tidy space. But when you're trying to create new habits—especially in a shared home—it helps to let the environment lead the way first. Once the behavior is established, you can always rework the setup to better match your vision. But in the beginning, the goal is follow-through. And follow-through thrives where friction is low.

Here are a few more simple tweaks that often help across the board:

- If baskets are being ignored, ditch the lids. No one wants to wrestle with a container just to toss in a baseball cap.
- If you're hearing "Where does this go?" on repeat, add a label. Even a sticky note helps.
- If drawers are becoming black holes, add dividers. Categories create visual order, which makes decisions easier and follow-through more likely.

When It's Not the Layout, It's the Habit

Even after you've adjusted the environment—moved the tray, added the hook, cleared the path—some habits die hard. If you've ever thought, *We literally set up a new spot for this, so why is it still landing on the counter?*, I hear you. In some cases, not only is environmental friction working against them, but also their autopilot.

That's when it helps to bring up OHIO: *Only Handle It Once*. This is one of the times a gentle conversation can be helpful. You're naming the habit and pointing to the easier alternative.

It might sound like, "Hey, I noticed your stuff's still landing on the counter even after we made the new drop zone. I totally get it; it's just habit. But part of what I'm working on is handling things once so they don't pile up. Would you be up for trying that too? I think of it as saving yourself from having extra work down the road. You do a little bit now so you won't have to clean up later, when you'd rather relax."

And when the environment is already supporting the new habit—short path, easy access, clear home—it makes follow-through that much easier. OHIO becomes less about effort and more about awareness. Because sometimes it's not the space; it's just an old pattern that needs a new cue.

Here's what this looks like in real life. One of my students lived with a friend who always left their water bottle and phone charger on the couch. Even after setting up a little tray on the side table, it kept happening. When she brought it up using the OHIO approach, her roommate said, "Oh, I just default to dropping them wherever I sit down." They added a second tray on the coffee table—right where the items usually landed—and that tiny shift worked.

Another student's partner had a habit of leaving laundry half folded on their bed, which would then get tossed to the floor at night. She gently said, "I've been trying this thing where I finish the task all at once—it saves me having to refold later. Want to try it with me?" Framing it as a shared effort (not a correction) helped them both finish the task more often.

Make Letting Go the Easiest Option for Clutter

Another way to set up your environment for success is setting up a Donation Station. Clutter doesn't always pile up because someone wants to keep everything; sometimes it lingers because there's no clear way out.

My student Carissa had spent years trying to get her husband to deal with the growing piles of clothes on and around his dresser. She asked, reminded, and tried organizing it for him numerous times. Nothing stuck.

Then one day, she placed a small donation bin right next to his dresser and said casually, "Hey, I put a bin here if there's anything you don't want anymore." No pressure or big talk.

That night the bin was full.

She realized that, throughout all those years, he hadn't truly been "resisting"; he just needed an option that made letting go feel easier and more obvious.

That tiny shift reduced the friction, and clearing a space

became simple. That's what the right environment does. It doesn't demand action; it invites it.

Try this:

- Place one bin in a spot where clutter tends to collect.
- Use what you already have: a box, basket, or bag works.
- Skip the speech (if you want). Throw out a casual, "Toss anything in here you don't need."
- Empty it when full or once a month, whatever fits your flow.

This isn't about asking someone to commit to a full declutter; it's just about getting started. You're helping them by making it easier to release what's ready to go. And sometimes that one small move is enough to shift the tone of your whole home.

The Psychology Behind the Donation Station

We've said before that the cause for clutter isn't always that people don't care; environmental friction or autopilot might be at play. Another cause is that many of us tend to postpone decisions. Studies have shown that chronic procrastination is one of the strongest predictors of clutter.[2] It's not sheer laziness. We tell ourselves, "I'll deal with it later," but later rarely comes. So piles start forming—on counters, in drawers, in garages—everywhere "someday" lives. A Donation Station interrupts that loop. Instead of waiting until the mood strikes, or someone has the time and energy to declutter, it offers a low-pressure "out" right in the moment. No decision fatigue or second-guessing. Just a small, visible exit ramp that makes letting go automatic.

The beauty here is that this doesn't require a spreadsheet or a complicated system. You just need one simple bin—and a spot that makes sense in their everyday flow. When the option is easy, follow-through happens. And when follow-through happens, the tension starts to lift.

In our home, the Donation Station was one of the first tools that got my husband and kids on board. I started with a bin in the garage, then I put one in each of our closets, the laundry room (perfect for outgrown kids' clothes), and even in my sons' bedrooms. No nagging. No pressure. Just an open invitation to release what was ready to go. Before long, those donation bins were filling up and our spaces were clearing out, little by little.

When You're Ready for the Conversation

Let's say you take these steps—you design for follow-through, you try out a new habit of OHIO, and you start using Donation Stations—and the tension is lingering. Maybe you're feeling stuck, emotions are running high, or you want to open the door to a more collaborative approach. In that case, another option is simply to have a calm, direct conversation. An honest exchange that can open the door to shared understanding and, maybe, even more shared action. Let's talk about ways to approach that.

To be clear, I'm not speaking as a family therapist or parenting expert here. I'm speaking as a decluttering expert and as a wife who's tried it all. Here's what I've tried with my husband, Andrew: Nagging? Check. Passive-aggressively slamming drawers? Yep. Flat-out telling him, "You need to get rid of your stuff"? Oh, I tried that too. None of those opened the door to real change.

What did work, along with the approaches we just talked about, were two things: discussing my Big Why with him and redefining what spaces were shared. No meltdowns required. Just a bit of strategy, clarity, and heart.

So, if you've tried all the things and still feel like you're hitting a wall, here are two conversation paths that tend to create more buy-in and less blowback. Try one, try both—whatever fits your dynamic best.

Share Your Big Why

If your partner doesn't understand why you want them to declutter—or what you're working toward—it's easy for them to tune out a request from you. It just feels like another task on their already-busy schedule. But when you start with the *why,* not the *what,* it invites more understanding.

This is about painting the picture before you ask for participation. You're saying, "Here's what I care about. Here's what I'm trying to change. And here's what could feel better—for both of us."

This might sound like, "I've realized that the house doesn't just feel messy—it feels heavy. It's draining my energy and I'm tired of being stressed out. I want our home to feel calmer and easier to manage. I'm not asking you to take everything on—but I'd love your support. And I know it could benefit both of us."

Sharing your Big Why helps your partner understand your motivation and helps them see what's in it for *them*: a clearer kitchen counter, a smoother morning routine, a home that doesn't feel like one big to-do list. This isn't about convincing them to want exactly what you want. It's about casting the vision, highlighting the benefits, and inviting them into it.

Define What's Shared—and What's Not

Sometimes the best way to reduce tension at home is to get clear on what's actually yours to manage. That's where this other conversational approach comes in: Define what space is their responsibility, what is yours, and what is shared.

When you feel responsible for decluttering their stack of paperwork or reorganizing their side of the closet, you'll feel more stressed. But, unless you live alone, you don't have to see yourself as responsible for every inch of your home. You also don't have to see everything in your home as a team project.

Instead, go to your partner or roommate and decide together:

- What are our shared zones—spaces we both use regularly and want to make function better?
- What are our personal zones—spaces we each get to manage on our own terms?

Shared zones might include kitchen counters, living room surfaces, the entryway or mudroom, closets, bathrooms, or laundry areas. These are the places where shared expectations can contribute to shared peace.

To address how you could manage those shared spaces together differently, you might say, "I've been thinking it might help if we talk about what areas we share and what we each want out of them. Like the kitchen counter—I'd love to keep it clear so I can prep dinner without moving stuff. Can we figure out a better spot for incoming mail or papers?"

You're inviting them to be part of the solution.

As for personal zones? That's their business. Even if it drives you slightly nuts that their desk is covered with random knickknacks or their nightstand is piled with books they never read, respecting those boundaries builds trust. Try to give yourself permission to overlook that space and release any concern about it. This approach creates breathing room for both of you—and helps you stay in your lane without giving up on shared progress.

As we wrap up this chapter, here's what I want you to know: You don't have to keep doing it all. You don't have to convince, nag, or wait for someone else to care as much as you do. You can start feeling better in your home before anyone else cares or is willing to change. And it won't happen through making demands more aggressively. Instead, try gentle, inviting conversations. Try adjusting the environment—put a hook by the door, a tray by the sink, or a Donation Station box next to an overflowing dresser. These things may seem small, but they invite action and follow-through.

In the next chapter, we'll build on this even more. You'll

learn how to help your entire household start noticing mess and building ownership over their things—so you're not the only one scanning the room, picking up the pieces, or holding the mental load.

Let's keep going.

REFLECT

- What would it feel like to stop doing it all yourself? To stop trying to convince someone else to care more—and instead shift your energy toward what you can influence? You don't need louder conversations or more frustration. You need small adjustments that support real follow-through. You need a way to protect your peace while still honoring the shared spaces you live in.
- What space feels the most tense in your home right now?
- And what's one environmental tweak—or one gentle conversation—you're now ready to try?

TAKE ACTION

Try one of the following this week to reduce friction and create more shared ease at home:

- Set up a Donation Station in a visible, high-traffic area. Keep it simple and casual, no speech required.

- Create a follow-through-friendly zone by placing a hook, tray, or basket where things are already landing, not where you wish they would.
- Use the OHIO principle to name and shift a habit. Pick one recurring drop zone and start practicing *Only Handle It Once.*
- Have a Big Why conversation. Focus on how you want your home to feel, not just what you want done.
- Define shared versus personal zones. Identify one shared space to co-manage and one personal zone to let go of.

Remember, you don't need perfect participation to make meaningful progress. You just need one small shift to start building momentum.

Chapter 11

Helping Kids Take Ownership

You've figured out your Stuff Story and decluttered. You've set up systems and started doing resets to keep your space running more smoothly. You've even found ways to invite another adult into the process. If you have kids, though, a problem likely remains: They're still causing a lot of work instead of joining in it.

You're constantly stumbling over their basketball shoes, LEGO pieces, or earbuds; one wrong step and it's a hop-on-one-foot, mutter-under-your-breath moment. At any given moment, you can find a backpack flung open, spilling notebooks and crumpled food wrappers like confetti.

Whether your kid is four or fourteen, their mess and clutter multiplies. And one of the biggest frustrations I hear from moms isn't just the stuff itself; it's feeling like their kids don't even notice or care about the messes.

You've probably already tried a few things:

- bribes or screen-time swaps ("If you clean up, you get fifteen more minutes . . .")
- pep talks and reminders
- consequences
- a chore list or chart with gold stars (that eventually gets ignored)
- frustrated lectures about responsibility

If none of that worked long-term, that's no surprise—lasting change doesn't come from pressure. It comes from ownership, which kids start to develop when they feel like a space belongs to them too.

That's what this chapter is about: helping your kids shift from "Just do what Mom says" to "This is my space too, and I know how to take care of it." What I'm sharing in this chapter is what I've seen work—over and over—for my students and in my own home. Here's how to develop shared responsibility and find a way forward that doesn't leave you carrying it all.

Teaching Kids to Notice and Reset

Some of our home cultures make mess easy to tune out. From an early age, kids learn to step over messes without even noticing them. Dirty clothes on the stairs, snack wrappers on the counter, toys in the hallway—it all blends into the background. Somewhere along the way, they picked up the message: *That's not my job. Someone else will handle it.* When that pattern repeats enough times, it becomes a belief.

In most homes, moms are doing the bulk of the chores and carrying the mental load—the scanning, anticipating, remembering, and managing that no one else sees. When that invisible load is unshared, the responsibility is unshared too.

That load will remain unshared and invisible as long as it goes unnoticed by others.

In *Fair Play*, a book about dividing home labor fairly, Eve Rodsky describes this load as "the sheer magnitude of the unseen, unacknowledged, unappreciated, and largely unpaid labor that mothers do."[1] If our kids can't see the mess, how can we expect them to clean it up? If they don't notice the clutter, how can they take ownership of it?

The first step to real change isn't more task lists or chore charts; it's awareness. The moment they start to see mess and clutter not as "Mom's problem" but as "part of our space to care for"—that's the beginning of shared ownership. Instead of demanding responsibility, you *teach them to notice*. You help them get to the point where they walk into a room, see a mess, and think, *I can do something about that*.

Here's how I started this process in my house.

One afternoon in the kitchen, I turned to my four-year-old son and asked, "What's one thing in this room that doesn't belong?"

He looked around, paused, and shrugged. "I don't see anything."

To me, it was glaring—a blanket on the floor, a cereal bowl from breakfast, scissors left on the counter.

So we started small. I gently pointed things out. "Do you

see that blanket in the middle of the floor? What about the cereal bowl on the table?"

Little by little, they started to notice on their own.

Teaching our kids to notice helps the home go from "Mom's job" to "our space." Building awareness lays the foundation for something better: ownership. If they don't have that, they'll never take initiative.

Noticing is the entry point. Ownership is the transformation.

One of the best tools I've found to bridge that gap is called the LAP Method. It's something I introduced to my kids after I taught them about resets (which we explored in chapter 3). Resets are how we manage expected mess. LAP is how I helped my kids do them.

The LAP Method: A Simple, Repeatable Reset

LAP is a three-step rhythm that helps kids take action instead of walking past what's out of place. It gives them a framework to see, decide, and follow through—without constant reminders. LAP stands for:

- **Look:** What's out of place?
- **Assess:** What is this thing? What needs to be done?
- **Put away:** Take action, and do it now.

When my kids started doing LAP, our house didn't magically become spotless. The practice did something better: It made the load feel shared. It also brought unexpected benefits, like fewer power struggles, more teamwork, and moments of genuine connection. Instead of throwing out constant reminders, I saw my kids take initiative. Instead of feeling alone in the mess, I started to feel supported. And they started to feel capable.

How to Teach LAP (Without Becoming the Cleanup Police)

Now that you know what LAP is, let's talk about how to teach it—without lectures, battles, or blank stares. This three-step process is simple enough for young kids to remember but powerful enough to build real ownership. Perfection isn't required for you to make progress. Keep it light, start small, and use everyday moments as practice.

Step 1: Look—What's Out of Place?

Teach your kids to scan the room like a detective looking for clues. Ask:

- "What doesn't belong here?"
- "Can you find something that's out of place on the floor, counter, or couch?"

With younger kids, make it playful:

- "How many stuffed animals are hiding in this room?"
- "Let's play I spy; can you find the mystery object on the floor?"

Tip: Start with one category at a time. This keeps the moment low-pressure and builds confidence without overwhelm.

Step Two: Assess—What Is This Thing?

This step builds the skill of discernment. Once they've spotted something, help them pause and think:

- Is it trash? (broken, empty, used)
- Is it clutter? (something we don't need, use, or love)
- Is it a keeper? (something that belongs but landed in the wrong spot)

Step Three: Put Away—Take Action

Now it's time to follow through:

- Trash goes in the bin.
- Clutter goes in the Donation Station.
- Keepers go back to their "homes."

With younger kids, you can make it fun:

- "Let's race—can you get it in the bin before I count to five?"
- "Where does this toy sleep at night?"
- "Your turn, my turn—let's tag-team this room!"

LAP doesn't just help kids pick up after themselves. It gives them a system to follow, decisions to make, and wins to feel proud of. And best of all? It takes the pressure off you to manage every step.

Making LAP a Habit

When LAP becomes part of your family's daily rhythm, tidying turns into something everyone just does. But here's the key: If LAP isn't anchored to a habit that's already happening, it will always feel like one more thing to remember, one more thing to cue. That's why the goal isn't just to teach LAP—it's to tie it to something predictable in your routine. Not a specific time of day but a transition your family moves through every day—like before meals, after returning home, and before bed.

These transitions are dependable, even if the clock isn't. Whether your kids get home from school at three thirty or seven o'clock after baseball or dance, dinner still happens. Bedtime still rolls around. When LAP is linked to those routines—not a rigid schedule—it's far more likely to stick.

Here are ways it could look.

- **Before meals.** Set a five-minute timer before dinner prep starts. Ask your child to "Take a LAP" around the playroom or main living area—books off the couch, toys back in bins, shoes by the door.
- **After school.** As soon as they walk in the door, use LAP as the transition cue: shoes off and lined up, backpacks hung up or unpacked, water bottles emptied and on the counter. Before they reach for snacks or screens, they've already completed a small reset.
- **Before bed.** Do a two-minute LAP in bedrooms or shared spaces: pajamas out, dirty clothes in the hamper, stuffed animals back in place, tech plugged in, books stacked neatly. Not perfect—just reset enough to start fresh the next day.

Growing Ownership Through LAP

Let's take a look at how this played out for one family. In this case, their daughter was five, but the same approach worked just as well later with their teenage son. The core idea is the same: Build awareness first, then support them as they take more ownership. What shifts with age isn't the strategy; it's how you apply it.

When I first spoke with my client Melanie, she was beyond frustrated. Every weekend, she found herself spending two hours cleaning up her five-year-old daughter Mia's room. Sorting through the mountain of stuffed animals, digging out dress-up clothes from under the bed, picking up tiny toy pieces one by one. But by midweek, it looked like nothing had even been done.

"I feel like her personal maid," Melanie told me. "I do all this work, and it's like she doesn't even care. It's exhausting." She'd tried it all: asking Mia to help, reward charts, even threatening to toss toys. But nothing changed, and resentment was building.

That's when we introduced LAP. We picked two anchor points for LAP resets:

- Before lunch: a reset in the play area
- Before bedtime: a wind-down reset in Mia's room

Beginning with the *Look* step, Melanie said to Mia, "Let's play detective. Can you find one thing that doesn't belong?"

This simple prompt helped Mia shift into engagement. She scanned the room, eyes lighting up, and proudly picked up a toy from the floor.

Melanie smiled. "Great job. Now let's figure out what it is."

As clinical psychologist Dr. Becky Kennedy teaches, connection—not control—is what makes real change possible with children. "When we're connected to our kids, so many things become easier. And when we're disconnected, so many things become harder."[2] When children feel seen and understood, their nervous system settles, and learning becomes possible.

Next came the *Assess* step. Instead of issuing commands, Melanie asked guiding questions: "What is this? Do we still use it?" and "Should this go back to its home, or can we let it go?" This is how kids develop discernment—not by being told what to do but by being supported while figuring it out.

This type of support is often called *scaffolding* in developmental psychology: offering just enough guidance to help a child stretch into a new skill without doing it for them.[3] Mia didn't need to clean her room alone. She needed someone beside her—coaching, not correcting.

Melanie also used Design for Follow-Through and tweaked the environment to help Mia succeed. She added picture labels to bins for dolls, books, and art supplies so Mia could follow visual cues instead of guessing. Melanie installed a low hook near the door where Mia could hang her backpack by herself and added a shallow basket near the art table for finished drawings.

These small changes reduced decision fatigue and boosted Mia's confidence during the final step, *Put Away,* because the systems made sense to her.

But the real shift came in how Melanie supported the process. She didn't swoop in or take over. Instead, she followed a hands-off approach while staying close, guiding with curiosity instead of correcting.

When Mia got stuck, Melanie would gently ask her, "Where do you think this lives?" "Should we tuck it into its bed for the night?" She invited participation instead of pushing for compliance.

As Dr. Becky says, "Connection is the foundation of cooperation. The more 'connection capital' you build, the more likely your child is to listen."[4] Melanie and Mia ultimately enjoyed not only a tidier room but a stronger bond.

With just two anchored LAP resets each day—one before lunch and one before bed—Mia's room became more manageable. Not because the mess stopped happening, but because ownership started growing. And Mia, at just five years old, was beginning to learn something powerful: *I can care for my space, and I know what to do.* She was developing not only a reset routine but a skill she could carry with her far beyond bedtime.

When Cleanup Becomes Second Nature

After a few weeks, Mia began resetting her room completely on her own. She still needed reminders here and there, but her space was clearer than ever—and Melanie was no longer pushing through two-hour cleaning sessions every weekend.

Even more? Decluttering conversations started to happen naturally.

One afternoon, Mia paused and held up a small teddy bear. "I don't really play with this one anymore," she said.

Then, without hesitation, she walked over to the Donation Station in the corner of her room and placed it inside—proudly.

Melanie didn't have to coax her or explain why it was time to let it go. Because Mia had been building the skill of managing her space, letting go came easier.

Of course, not every child will part with toys as easily. Some kids are naturally more sentimental, and that's okay. Everyone understands in their own time.

So to start, keep the focus on LAP and the rhythm of

resets. When the foundation is strong, the rest will follow—at their pace, in their way. No pressure, just steady progress, one LAP at a time.

LAP and Neurodivergence

After seeing how well LAP worked with Mia, Melanie knew it had potential for her fourteen-year-old son, Jackson, too.

Jackson's room was overwhelming, with piles of clothes, tangled chargers, water bottles, and school papers everywhere. Any of his attempts to clean up usually ended in shutdown. An ADHD diagnosis helped explain some of those moments; he wasn't being defiant. He was overloaded.

Melanie didn't need a new system. She needed to adapt LAP a bit more to meet Jackson where he was.

So she started with one category: trash.

"Let's just look for trash," she said. "That's it. No organizing. No decluttering."

Instead of using a timer (which Mia loved but Jackson found overwhelming), she played his favorite music in the background. The rhythm gave him something to focus on while they picked up. She stayed close—not to manage every move, but to support him, offer encouragement, and help him stay focused on the task. This technique—known as *body doubling*—is often helpful for ADHD brains.[5]

And it worked. They made a little progress, enough that Jackson didn't shut down.

The next day, they tackled another category: paper.

Jackson looked around and groaned, "I don't know what to do with all these school papers."

That's when Melanie realized that he truly wasn't avoiding the mess. He just didn't know where things were supposed to go. So she grabbed two bins and set them on his desk. One for temporary papers, like unfinished homework or notes he still needed. One for longer-term keeps, like drawings or graded assignments he was proud of.

When he picked up a stray worksheet, she asked, "Do you need this for school, or can we recycle it?"

Some decisions were quick. Others took more time. "You don't have to decide right now," she'd say gently. "Let's put it in your keep bin and revisit it later." That one sentence made all the difference.

By honoring his need for processing time—and giving him a clear structure instead of vague instructions—Melanie helped Jackson access the skills he already had. He wasn't avoiding the task anymore; he was learning how to navigate it and growing in confidence.

Creating Space for Ownership

As resets became more natural, Melanie introduced one final step.

"I put a donation bin in your closet," she told Jackson. "If you find anything you don't want anymore, you can drop it in there."

At first, the bin sat empty. But a few weeks later, while

putting books away, Jackson paused. He picked up an old hoodie he didn't wear anymore and placed it in the bin. A few days later, it was an old phone case. Then an old comic book.

No reminders. No pressure. Just readiness—and the right system to support it.

What changed? The environmental influence of the donation bin helped decluttering become a choice, not a pressured chore. And Jackson was learning to make that choice on his own.

A month later, Melanie walked past his room and paused. For the first time in a long time, she didn't see piles of wrappers or papers stacked like Jenga towers. The space wasn't spotless—there was still a sock on the floor and a book leaning against the bed—but it was manageable. Peaceful, even.

He'd picked up a few things before bed. He'd dropped unused toys into the bin when he felt ready. He'd done a quick LAP before playing video games—not because she told him to, but because he felt the difference.

But the biggest shift wasn't in what he did—it was in how he felt.

He was sleeping better. Finding things faster. Experiencing firsthand how much easier life is when your room doesn't feel like a mental minefield. That's the quiet magic of LAP.

Jackson had been overwhelmed by the number of micro-decisions his messy room demanded. And like so many kids—especially those with neurodivergences—he hadn't been taught a doable approach.

As Dr. Thomas Brown, clinical psychologist and leading ADHD researcher, explains, executive function is "the brain's management system"—the set of mental skills that allows us to start tasks, stay organized, manage frustration, and see things through to completion.[6] Brown emphasizes that kids with executive function challenges aren't lazy or defiant. Instead, they often struggle with "activation"—in his words, "getting started on a task, even a task they recognize as very important to them, until the very last minute."[7]

That's why tools like LAP are so powerful. By helping with "activation," you give kids a starting point, a sense of sequence, and a concrete way to follow through—which is game-changing for those whose brains freeze when the mess feels too big.

LAP as a Family: Shared Resets in the Home

As Jackson became more confident managing his room and Mia kept using LAP in her Daily Resets, Melanie realized they were ready to expand the practice beyond their personal spaces.

One night after dinner, she said casually, "Before we head upstairs, let's take a LAP in the kitchen and living room."

So Jackson wiped the counters. Mia put her school artwork away. Melanie loaded the dishwasher.

It took ten minutes. But in that time, it was no longer Melanie versus the mess. It was the family working together.

They did the same thing after dinner the next night, then the next—before long, it became a routine. Some nights were fun and upbeat; others were quiet and begrudging. But the rhythm stuck.

Melanie's story might look different from yours. Maybe your kids are younger, or maybe they're older and the clutter looks more like laundry piles, crumpled hoodies, or hair tools left all over the bathroom counter. No matter how old your child is, this still applies. With younger kids, it might look like clearing toys. With teens, it might mean managing schoolwork or sports gear. But the goal is the same: Teach them how to notice, decide, and take action. When the rhythm is simple and repeatable, your kids will surprise you.

If you're reading this and thinking, *That feels so far from where we are*, that's okay. You can start wherever you are and take little steps toward these rhythms over time. Some families start with LAP in a shared space, like the living room or kitchen. Others begin by helping their kids use it in their bedroom or playroom. There's no wrong way to start. Just pick the spot that feels easiest or most compelling—and build from there.

And remember, LAP isn't only about cleaning up. It's about raising kids who learn to notice what needs attention, take ownership of their space, and follow through. And whether your child is five or fifteen, those are skills that will serve them in partnerships, friendships, future jobs, and every home they'll live in after yours.

You're not only teaching them how to tidy a room. You're helping them build the confidence to take responsibility, the awareness to see what needs care, and the resilience to follow through—especially when it's not fun or easy. That's brave work. And it starts in the everyday moments.

I am so proud of you for leading this simplicity movement in your family. I know it takes effort, and I also know it will be worth it.

TAKE ACTION

Whether you're raising toddlers, parenting tweens, or tackling shared spaces with grown-ups, the LAP Method gives everyone in your home a simple, repeatable way to notice, decide, and take action.

Pick a single area to introduce LAP—your child's room or a shared space like the kitchen. Keep it small and manageable.

Look: What's out of place?

- Scan the space.
- Pick one item to start with.
- Use playful prompts with younger kids: "Can you find one thing that doesn't belong?"

Assess: What is it?

- Is it trash, clutter, or something we use and love?
- Help your kids name what they see before jumping to action.
- Give grace and guidance—some decisions take practice.

Put Away: Where does it go?

- Take one small action to restore order.
- Use labeled bins or clear categories to build confidence.
- Make it light and quick—especially during transition points like bedtime or before meals.

After your child does this the first time, make it a practice by anchoring LAP to a daily routine. Tie it to natural transitions—before meals, after school, or before bed—so it becomes a predictable habit instead of a chore.

Also, make it a shared experience. Model LAP yourself, then invite your family to join. Keep it short, use music, or turn it into a game. Don't demand perfection; invite participation.

Chapter 12

Break the Shopping-and-Clutter Cycle

"Where did the money go, Katy?"

My husband was holding the credit card statement, and I couldn't give him an answer. I stood there frozen, cheeks flushed, a familiar pit in my stomach. On the counter behind him was a stack of unopened Amazon boxes I'd been collecting for days, maybe weeks. I had planned to open them when no one was home, sneak the contents into closets or drawers, and casually deflect if he noticed anything new.

"This old thing? Nah, I've had it forever," I might try.

But in that moment, the game was up. The soft tap of the credit card bill landing on the table was louder than anything he said.

I wasn't buying luxury handbags or redoing the kitchen. It was a bunch of little things, twelve dollars here, twenty-seven dollars there. A candle that promised calm, another planner I swore would finally make me feel on top of things. A Target run that turned into a cart full of "treats."

It all added up—to clutter, yes.

More than that, it added up to avoidance. I wasn't shopping for stuff; I was shopping for peace. Relief. A sense of control in a season when everything felt out of my hands. But the more I bought, the worse it got. More stuff, more guilt and shame. More hiding packages and hoping deliveries wouldn't come when he was home. More clutter in my home, the very thing I was working so hard to fight against.

Until one afternoon, sitting at the kitchen table with that bill in front of me, I broke. Tears welled up in my eyes as I whispered the words I had been avoiding for years: "I think . . . I have a shopping problem."

In that season, everything felt like too much. I was home with young kids, trying to keep everything running while falling apart inside. The shopping wasn't about the stuff—it was about giving myself *something* to look forward to. A hit of hope. A tiny win. I didn't have the language for it then, but I was spending to feel like I had some semblance of control. To feel like I mattered. Like I was doing something *for me*—even if it came wrapped in shame.

That moment in the kitchen led me to realize something important: The clutter in my home didn't start with the *stuff*; it started with the *spending.*

And here's what made it even harder to admit: I was already deep into my decluttering journey. I had no trouble calling out my husband for his clutter, or my kids' toy overflow, or the garage stuff we'd moved cross-country more times than I could count. I could spot clutter more easily, but I hadn't looked at *myself.* While I put a lot of focus on what needed to go, I was still bringing things in, constantly.

I was decluttering with one hand while shopping with the other.

And the spending pattern was poking holes in everything I was trying to build.

I didn't understand it then, but what I was doing was a type of self-protective reaction; my brain was trying to help me cope. Once I started learning what was happening under the surface, everything began to make more sense, and I was finally able to build healthier spending habits. That season helped me realize something bigger: It's not just what we declutter that shapes our homes. It's what we choose to bring in. And that's where this chapter comes in.

Even if your spending habits look different from mine—whether you shop out of boredom, stress, habit, or not much at all—this chapter will help you zoom out and take stock. It's not about assigning guilt; it's about getting curious: What role does shopping play in your life right now? What kind of energy are you inviting into your home with the things you purchase? This chapter will help you build that awareness, recognize unhelpful patterns, and move toward a version of shopping that supports—not sabotages—the simpler, more intentional life you're creating.

Your Brain on Shopping Carts

If you've ever clicked "Add to Cart" faster than you could blink, only to wonder later why you bought yet another version of something you already had—congratulations, you're human. In those kinds of moments, your brain is doing exactly what it was built to do: release dopamine. It does it every time you shop—in fact, it does it even before you click "Buy Now."

Many people think of dopamine as the "pleasure chemical," but it's not about feeling satisfied. It's about *craving*. As neuroscientist Dr. Andrew Huberman has explained, dopamine is the "molecule of motivation" because it's released in *anticipation* of a reward—not in the experience of the reward itself.[1] That hopeful feeling of "maybe this will finally fix it" or "this will help me get it together" is dopamine at work, and it's driving you to pursue.

This is why "adding to cart" feels good. It's why getting a tracking number brings a spark of energy or a package on your porch feels like progress, even if what's inside doesn't solve anything.

But we all know how the story ends. The hit is short-lived, the novelty fades, and, without you realizing it, your brain goes looking for the next one.

And here's the kicker: You can't *not* get that hit. It's automatic. It's physiological. Even the most die-hard minimalists—the kind who could fit their entire life into a backpack—still feel that rush. So this isn't an issue of self-control; it's simply brain chemistry.

This is why even the best-laid plans fall apart. While budgets work for many people, they often aren't built for what we're up against today. With 24-7 access to online shopping, one-click checkouts, and endless "get it now" messages, we're navigating an environment that's designed to overstimulate our brains and pull our attention in a hundred directions. That's why so many smart, capable women set a spending limit—and still find themselves opening Amazon boxes two days later, wondering, *How did that happen again?* Even with the best intentions, our modern environment is stacked against us.

Dr. Kent Berridge, a leading neuroscientist in reward systems, has explained another interesting complexity in how our brains work: Wanting and liking are actually separate systems. That means we can crave something without actually enjoying it—or enjoy something without actively craving it. These two processes happen in different parts of the brain and are powered by different chemicals.[2] So if you've ever wanted something badly, only to feel disappointed once you had it (or felt "meh" once the package arrived), that's not you being irrational or broken—it's your brain doing exactly what it's wired to do. And here's the kicker: The brain prefers the *chase*. It's more motivated by the pursuit than the actual reward. Which explains why the thrill of clicking "Add to Cart" often fades faster than we expect.

Again, this isn't a moral failure or a character flaw; it's your reward system doing what it's designed to do.

And modern marketing? Oh, it knows that well, my friend. It's engineered to hijack that exact loop, so you'll chase that feeling again and again.

The Game Is Rigged (But You Can Learn the Rules)

Modern marketing doesn't just hope you'll buy items; it's designed to make you *feel* like you need to.

Teams of behavioral scientists and neuromarketing

experts are studying how your brain reacts to urgency, scarcity, beauty, and belonging. They test everything—from the color of the Buy Now button to the phrasing in your favorite influencer's caption. So your inbox ends up full of discounts as well as emotional triggers dressed up as convenience.

Those countdown timers, "Only three left" messages, "Run, don't walk" captions—those are not accidental. They're intentional. They tap into your brain's fear of missing out, not just on the item but on the *version of life* it promises. Maybe it's a better morning routine, a calmer home, a more confident version of yourself. When those promises come wrapped in emotional language—or endorsed by someone you admire—it doesn't register as marketing. It feels like truth, like urgency, like your next right move.

The wild part? Most of this happens without you even realizing it. Your brain is wired to mirror what it sees—especially when it encounters something that seems happy, successful, or "put together." So when someone you follow shares their skincare routine or their perfectly organized pantry, your brain sees a path to a version of life you want.

That's not weakness. That's biology.

And marketers are banking on it.

We're Not Just Buying Products

We've now looked at the role dopamine plays and how marketers push our buttons, and we've touched on the fact that beneath the science is something far more personal:

When we buy products, we're buying possibilities—stories, solutions, beliefs, transformations, identities, and emotions we want to feel. This is worth digging into and exploring further, because it'll play a critical role in helping you gain awareness of your individual experience with spending.

When you buy a new moisturizer, you're buying not only a blend of oils and ingredients but also the *hope* that you'll look in the mirror and feel more at ease. Maybe you'll see someone who is glowing, radiant, pulled-together; someone who looks rested, worthy, beautiful. Maybe this kind of skin will give you the confidence to show up fully and be seen without shrinking. You, at last, might stop hiding behind layers of self-doubt and speak without second-guessing.

You're not just buying skincare. You're buying the transformation from insecure to confident, from invisible to radiant, from never enough to *finally okay.*

It's rarely about the thing itself. It's about what we hope it will *change*—about us.

You don't just buy leggings. You buy the belief that you're finally going to "get it together." That this is the week you'll become the version of yourself who works out, who drinks water, who feels good in her own skin. You don't just buy a candle. You buy calm, comfort, and control. Each purchase is a micro-attempt to become who we think we *should* be or who, maybe deep down, we truly *want* to be, or simply how we want to feel.

The more we feel like we're not enough as we are, the more susceptible we are to the pitch.

Want to feel like the best version of yourself? There's a

sixty-eight-dollar supplement, a matching workout set, and a protein shaker for that.

Want to feel on top of things for once? Download the seven-dollar app, refill your water bottle, and order that fourth organizing bin—it'll definitely help this time.

Want to feel like the "together mom"? Just grab the bento lunchbox and commit to a ten-step morning routine. Easy, right?

Every ad, email, and influencer caption is reinforcing the same belief: You're not quite there yet. You're missing something, and this product is the fix.

When we step back and look at it all, it seems pretty black and white. Why would we ever fall for this? (Especially when we know about the dopamine release and the marketing tricks!) It's because we care—we want to be better partners, parents, friends. We want to feel calm, collected, worthy. So we walk into a trap that says, *This product will deliver worthiness. This package will fix the ache underneath*.

This is how clutter grows silently, not only in our homes, but in our minds. When the promise doesn't deliver, we don't stop buying—we just start searching harder. From there, a cycle is formed and continues indefinitely.

When spending becomes automatic—when it starts to feel like the answer to everything—that's when it's worth looking even deeper. Let's consider what we might be truly searching for on the inside before we reach for another solution outside ourselves.

The Emotional Roots of Spending

We're going to explore how shopping can be wrapped up in emotions, but before we do, let's get one thing straight: Not *all* shopping is deeply emotional. Not every Target run is a cry for help. Not every new pair of leggings or planner is revealing some hidden issue. Sometimes we shop because we need things or because we *like* things (that's allowed)! We want to enjoy life, express our style, or prepare for what matters most. There's nothing wrong with that, and there's a place for enjoying a little retail therapy from time to time.

But other times something deeper is driving us, and becoming more self-aware empowers us to take good care of ourselves.

For most women I've worked with—including myself—spending isn't random. It's emotional and it's deeply personal. We can use shopping as a way to cope with feelings we don't know how to process—or were never taught to sit with in the first place.

We sometimes shop because we feel:

- anxious and want to soothe ourselves
- overwhelmed and want to feel in control
- lonely and want to feel connected or cared for
- inadequate and want to prove we're enough
- bored
- angry
- tired of trying so hard in other areas of life (and this one little thing feels like a reward we deserve)

When you've been taught to push through, smile through, keep going no matter what, spending can become your fastest, most accessible relief valve. And it does work—for a moment.

If you're starting to feel like I'm piling on the blame—trust me, I'm not. Remember my story at the beginning of this chapter? There's no judgment here. Only the invitation to become more and better equipped to give yourself care.

When you can name what you're truly craving—peace, presence, belonging—you can begin to give yourself those things without asking your cart to carry the weight.

The Pause Plan: A New Way to Shop (or Not Shop)

Now that we've got a handle on what's going on when we shop—our brain activity, the marketing schemes, and our emotions and longings driving us—it's time to look at new strategies we can bring to our spending decisions.

While you can't control the initial dopamine release, you *can* interrupt the loop that follows.

While you can't escape the marketing games, you don't have to keep playing along.

And yes, you might have anxiety, overwhelm, boredom, loneliness, or the sense that you're not enough as you are, but you don't have to try to address your needs with purchases.

With greater awareness about what's at play internally and externally, you can pause, get curious about the pull you're feeling, and make choices from a place of *clarity*—not pressure.

No need to shame yourself into better behavior. You just need to notice, pause, and choose with intention. And the Pause Plan can help you do it.

Step One: Notice the Cue

You can't shift what you don't see, so you need to learn to notice the cue that gets you thinking seriously about a purchase. It's often embedded with your environment and habits; the internal and external environments work together, training you to reach for a fix. This includes the apps you open without thinking and the emails that flood your inbox, or the way you might use shopping as a break, a treat, or a coping mechanism that's only ever one tap away.

Once you spot the scenario and thoughts that prompt you to click "Add to Cart," you can keep your eye out for it when it comes again. And when it does, you can gently ask yourself, *What's really going on here?*

Are you feeling anxious? Bored? Behind? Out of control? Or did something in your environment—an email, a scroll, a stressful moment—flip on the autopilot?

For me, I used to scroll online toward the end of the day, right around the time my brain felt like mush and I was mentally tapped out. Between the toddler meltdowns, the diaper blowouts, and trying to figure out what was for dinner, shopping became a fast escape hatch. It gave me a moment of relief when everything else felt chaotic. Sometimes I didn't even notice I was doing it.

But once I started recognizing that cue, I began changing the environment around me so I could calm what was happening inside me.

I got up off the couch. I put on music. I did a few jumping jacks or walked into a different room or stepped outside with the kids to play in the front yard. I interrupted the pattern before it swept me away.

That's what this step is about. Not guilt or rigid rules. Just awareness—and a willingness to pause long enough to choose something else. Because clarity is always the first kind of courage.

Step Two: Create Space

Shame rushes. Self-trust slows down.

Between the urge and the action, there's a sliver of space, and that's where your power lives.

This is where you pause. You breathe. You remind yourself you don't need to act on the feeling right away. So you'll just notice it, sit with it, and give it room to settle.

Here's what this looks like for me: When I'm online, I screenshot the item instead of buying it, and then I wait forty-eight hours. Ninety-nine percent of the time, I don't want it anymore. Sometimes I'll scroll back through the photos and think, *Seriously, Katy? That was almost a purchase?* (Bad fashion choices have been made, my friend.)

This approach is sort of the inverse of the Time Will

Tell Box we've discussed before. Not sure if you need an item in your space? Give it some time, and you'll find out. It sounds so simple—but it really works. We don't need more complicated systems or ironclad rules. We just need more breathing room between the feeling and the action.

In-store? Same idea. I've walked around with something in my cart before and told myself, *If I still want this next week, I can come back.* Spoiler alert: I never go back. That physical pause—just walking away—is often enough to reset the urgency. And if I feel myself getting swept up in a sale or "But it's such a good deal!" moment, I ask myself, *Would I pay full price for this?*

If the answer is no, that tells me something. It reminds me that I'm more drawn to the deal than to the item itself. Because the real cost of something isn't always on the price tag. It's in the space it takes up, the guilt it brings, or the emotional weight it adds later.

Those two days, or two aisles in the store, give my nervous system a chance to come back online. And then I get to choose with more intention.

Step Three: Meet the Need Without the Cart

By now, you've noticed the urge and named it. You've paused instead of reacting. Next, it's time to meet the real need—the one the purchase was never going to fully satisfy.

Again—this bears repeating—what we're longing for most is the *hope* a purchase or an item will make us feel, not the thing itself.

So instead of asking, *Should I buy this?* try asking, *What am I really needing right now—and how can I give that to myself in a way that lasts?*

If you're craving a sense of control, tidy one drawer or small surface. Create order where you are.

If you're feeling invisible or not enough, text someone who truly sees you or reread a kind message from a friend.

If you're feeling anxious or out of sorts, step outside. Breathe. Stretch. Reconnect to your body.

These aren't substitutes; they're more effective ways to address your deeper needs. You aren't denying yourself beauty or joy; you're steering yourself toward life-giving experiences, the kind a product can't offer.

When you use the Pause Plan, you'll be interrupting the dopamine loop, outsmarting the marketing ploys, and avoiding clutter. But more importantly, you'll be becoming the kind of woman who knows how to take care of herself even in the hard moments. That's the work. That's the shift.

What I Wish I Knew Then

Looking back now, I have such empathy for the woman who used to hide Amazon boxes in the back of closets and pray deliveries didn't come when anyone else was home. That version of me was just trying to cope with an overstimulating environment in the most hardwired way. But she didn't realize that every click and impulse buy was pulling her further away from the kind of life she wanted.

At the time, I said I wanted a calmer home and more presence with my kids—but my spending told a different story. I kept bringing in more stuff, hoping it would give me energy, comfort, or a sense of control. Instead, it added visual clutter, financial stress, and more things to manage. The gap between the life I said I wanted and the life I was creating kept widening. And it was in that space—in the discomfort of that disconnect—that something shifted. I began asking better questions. I began listening more closely to what I really needed. I began stepping closer to my values, my vision, my Big Why, one choice at a time.

As I gained clarity, the fears about "getting caught" or "messing up again" loosened their grip. Little by little, I tried to stop managing my feelings with shopping and instead meet my needs with honesty, compassion, and intention.

Was it a smooth, easy path? Nope. It took time, focus, and grace each time I fell back into a well-worn habit. I found, over time, that it was enough to change everything.

If no one's told you lately, it is okay that you feel the urge to spend or that you struggle to stick to a budget. You're not weak for falling into a pattern you don't want to continue. If you're even acknowledging any of this is your experience, you're brave for naming it and courageous for wanting more. And you're strong enough to choose a different way—one small pause at a time.

Freedom doesn't always look dramatic; it often shows up in the messy in-between.

It's the moment you delete a promo email without even opening it. It's the pause before you add something to your cart—then the decision not to add it. It's walking through Target and feeling the pull but walking past the cute clothes anyway. It's being able to scroll online without spiraling or open your bank app without that familiar pit in your stomach.

It's more space in your closet, more peace in your mind, and more confidence in your choices—because they're aligned. It's noticing a hard day and reaching for something real instead of something wrapped in plastic or delivered to your door.

That's the kind of freedom you're creating here. It'll bring you steady, grounding peace that lasts.

The Work Beneath the Cart

As we close out this chapter I want to remind you that the first powerful step you can take is simply paying attention. That matters more than you know. You'll be making progress if you see the pattern and realize you can choose differently than you have before—then pass on the purchase, even just once.

You don't have to become someone who never shops or never slips. If you make choices that you later consider to be mistakes, that's okay. You'll transform through self-compassion and clarity, not the absence of mistakes.

So just keep practicing pausing, over and over again.

Every time you get curious about an urge instead of reacting to it, you'll build trust in yourself. You'll plant and nurture the kind of roots that no receipt, return policy, or sale could ever offer. And as you start establishing habits of turning to other things than shopping to meet your needs, you'll feel the peace that comes with having less decluttering to do (the benefit of having less coming in!) and knowing how to nourish yourself.

REFLECT

See if you can pin down what sometimes drives your urge to buy something.

- boredom
- stress
- loneliness
- a craving for control
- a need to feel seen or valued

Maybe it's something else. Whatever it is, try to name the feeling underneath the scroll or the cart. No shame, just curiosity. The more awareness you bring to your patterns, the more power you'll have to shift them.

Think about a recent purchase, or one you're considering now. Ask yourself:

- *What am I really hoping this gives me?*
- *What do I think it will solve or soothe?*

Consider what other ways you could give yourself care apart from making a purchase.

- When life feels heavy, what helps you feel lighter—besides buying something?
- When you're overwhelmed, what actually brings you calm?
- When you're craving connection, how else might you reach for it?
- When you want to feel seen, how can you acknowledge yourself without needing a package on your doorstep?

TAKE ACTION

Try making a list of go-to practices or rituals that fill you up in a lasting way. Keep it somewhere visible, so next time you're tempted to click "Buy Now," you can turn to something that truly supports you instead.

Also, before your next purchase, pause. Instead of asking, *Should I buy this?* try asking, *What am I actually needing right now—and is this the best way to meet that need?* Write the question on a sticky note. Put it on your laptop, in your wallet, or inside the console of your car. Let it be a gentle nudge that brings you back to yourself.

Chapter 13

No More Burnout: Tools That Keep You Going

I've always loved the story of the tortoise and the hare. Not because it's about winning, but because it's about how we keep going.

If you haven't heard it in a while, here's the short version: The speedy, overconfident hare challenges the slow-moving tortoise to a race. The hare takes off in a flash, certain he'll win. The tortoise never tries to match his speed; she just keeps walking, one step at a time. And in the end? She crosses the finish line first. Not because she was fast, but because she never stopped.

What sticks with me most is that the tortoise showed up at all. She didn't wait until she felt ready or tell herself she wasn't cut out for it. She accepted her pace and kept moving.

Do we do the same when we feel behind?

We often approach decluttering with hare energy: ambitious, excited, ready to overhaul everything. *This time, I'll overhaul the whole house,* we think. *I'll wake up earlier. I'll finally get my life together.*

And maybe for a little while, we do. Then life happens.

A trip throws us off, a few late nights leave us sleep deprived, the to-do list triples. Or we walk into a cluttered space and feel inexplicably paralyzed. *I can't keep up. I'm too tired. I've lost momentum.* We wonder if we ever had it in the first place.

But here's the truth: What looks like failure might just be feedback.

Maybe fast and frantic wasn't your best rhythm. Maybe the tortoise didn't win in spite of her slowness, but because of it.

That kind of steady, imperfect, quiet persistence is what this chapter is about. Because momentum doesn't come from speed; it comes from showing up.

You don't need a five-hour window or a viral before-and-after to make real change. You need a way to keep going when life gets "lifey." When your schedule shifts, your mood dips, or your kid gets sick again. This chapter isn't just about routines—it's about resilience. It's about having tools that work for you when things aren't working perfectly and showing yourself that steady is still success.

Let's walk through a few tools that make that possible. Remember: You don't need a big leap. You just need a next right step.

What If Small Is the Strategy?

At the beginning of this book, we talked about how our Stuff Story shapes our relationship with things. But it also shapes our relationship with progress. We've absorbed decades of cultural messaging that says change should be big and dramatic. A closet purge! A full-house transformation! The twelve-hour weekend blitz! But most of us? We're not living inside a makeover montage. We're living in real life.

We're juggling meetings, parenting, fatigue, and invisible labor. We don't have six uninterrupted hours; we've got ten distracted minutes. And when all we've seen modeled is big, bold, and perfect, ten minutes feels like nothing. One drawer feels like a drop in the bucket.

But what if it's not?

Priya, a podcast listener from Oregon, shared that for weeks she avoided starting because she didn't think her effort would be "enough." She didn't have time to declutter a whole room or even an hour to spare. But one night, while clearing the dinner dishes, she spotted a pile of takeout menus and junk mail that had been sitting on the counter for weeks. On impulse, she recycled the whole stack.

"It felt ridiculously small," she said, "but the next morning, that clear spot made me feel a little more in control. And for the first time, I wanted to do more."

That's what a single step can do—it proves movement is possible, even when momentum feels far away.

So what if "just doing the small things" isn't second best but the actual strategy?

Here's what I tell my students all the time: Real change doesn't have to be sweeping. It just has to be repeatable. It has to be something you'll actually come back to. That means honoring the few minutes you do have. Tossing one thing and calling that a win. Resetting a counter and letting that be enough. These aren't scraps of progress; they're seeds.

Because when you repeat those small moments? They stack. You start to feel lighter. Not in a TikTok before-and-after way, but in a deep, personal, sustainable way.

Clutter Audits—Progress in Real Time

We'll start with Clutter Audits, which are small decisions you make in any given moment of your day. No big setup, no hours blocked off. Just a quick, intentional choice to let go of what no longer serves you.

Too many of us wait until closets are bursting or counters are buried before we tackle clutter, then spend hours tearing through piles until we're exhausted. Clutter audits break that cycle. They work in the background of your daily routine, helping you make progress and stay on top of what you've already cleared—so clutter never has the chance to pile up in the first place.

You're brushing your teeth and notice a skincare product you never use. You're putting away laundry and see a shirt your kid has outgrown. You're unloading groceries and toss the expired flyer that's been sitting on your counter. That's a Clutter Audit. It's not a new task on your list. It's a shift in how you do what you're already doing, just with more intention.

Here's how it works: As you move through your day, scan for what you consistently skip or avoid. When you spot something that isn't serving you, apply the Opportunity Rule

(Have I had the chance to use this in the last six months?). Then immediately move it to your donation station. Don't set it aside "for later." Handle it now, then keep moving.

These moments don't interrupt your day; they're built into it. And over time, they change the way you see your space. You stop waiting for the perfect moment and start making small, honest decisions right when they show up. These moments might not look like progress from the outside, but they're how your home learns a new rhythm. And how you do too.

25 to Thrive: Bigger Wins on Your Terms

Once you've started responding to clutter in real time, there will be moments when you have more energy or a larger pocket of time and want to go a little deeper. That's where 25 to Thrive comes in.

Set a timer for twenty minutes. Pick a small area—a shelf, drawer, or bin—and start decluttering. Don't overthink. Don't overplan. Just move.

Then set five more minutes to reset. Bag the donations. Toss the trash. Wipe down the surface. Put things away.

This practice works because it taps into what research confirms: Our brains make faster, clearer decisions in short bursts. Beyond twenty-five minutes, decision fatigue sets in and momentum dips. But inside that focused window, we get into flow. We finish things.[1]

My student Melissa felt stuck for months, waiting for the perfect time to deal with her hallway closet. But after a few weeks of Clutter Audits, she felt ready for more. One night, with dinner in the oven and her kids occupied, she grabbed a timer and chose a single shelf. Twenty-five minutes later, she had cleared cords, crushed gift bags, dead batteries, and duplicate clutter. It wasn't a full overhaul. It was one solid win.

Later that night, she messaged me: "It felt like I followed through on something I've been putting off for years."

That's the beauty of 25 to Thrive. It's not about doing it all; it's about making progress that's visible, meaningful, and doable. It's a boost for your belief: *I can do this.* And belief is what fuels everything that follows.

Another client, Erika, keeps a sticky note by her sink that simply says "25 to Thrive." It's her reminder that if she finds a pocket of time between Zoom calls or after dinner, she can reclaim just one space. She's not decluttering full rooms; she's building trust.

"It's like investing in future me," she said. "Even twenty-five minutes makes me feel like I showed up."

When Overwhelm Hits (Because It Will)

Even with the best tools and intentions, there will still be days when you feel completely stuck. You open a closet or look at a space and feel your whole body resist. That doesn't mean you're doing it wrong; it means your brain is trying to protect you from overload. Sometimes, clutter isn't the cause of that overload; it's the final straw.

Research shows the average person makes up to

thirty-five thousand decisions per day.[2] For women juggling households, careers, and caregiving, that number feels even higher. Every "What's for dinner?" "Did I reply to that email?" or "Who's driving to practice?" stacks on top of your brain's already-full load. Add in a cluttered room, and suddenly every item is another decision your brain can't make.

Where does this go?

Should I keep this?

What if I need it?

Our brains reach capacity and shut down. Not because we're lazy, but because we're trying to survive.

When that happens, don't push harder.

Shift strategies.

Overwhelm Off-Ramp 1: The Zen Zone

When your environment is working against your nervous system, try making the decisions somewhere *away* from the mess, somewhere calmer. This is what led me to create something I now call the Zen Zone.

At first, it was one small corner of our bedroom. Instead of standing in the chaos of the closet trying to make fifty decisions at once, I'd bring a few items into that calmer space—a handful of swimsuits, a drawer's worth of clothes, one small pile I was ready to face. That shift changed everything. I didn't need more motivation. I needed fewer distractions.

Here's why it works: When we walk into a room with high visual volume—think boxes stacked to the ceiling, mixed categories, overflowing bins—our brains register every item as input. I've worked with clients who couldn't even open the door to certain rooms—not because they weren't capable, but because standing in the doorway made their chests tighten and their brains shut down. That's how powerful our environment is. It's not about motivation; it's about mental load. Each visible object adds to it. That's why we can feel our shoulders tighten or our heart race when we step into an overstuffed space.

Studies show that clutter increases cortisol, the stress hormone.[3] It's not in your head; your body is responding to overwhelm in real time.

The Zen Zone strategy can be especially helpful for those who are neurodivergent or highly sensitive. A calm, clear space gives your brain fewer inputs to filter, making it easier to focus, decide, and regulate. So instead of trying to make dozens of decisions in the middle of all that, the Zen Zone gives you a place to breathe first. It calms your nervous system so you can think more clearly and act more confidently.

You don't need a spare room. You don't even need a whole corner. You just need one area that feels clear enough to think:

- a clean table in the kitchen
- a chair in your bedroom
- a small patch of floor by a window
- a landing at the top of the stairs
- even a tray or box lid you carry from room to room (consider it a "portable Zen Zone")

If you live in a multilevel home, choose (or create) one calm space on each floor. If you're in a smaller apartment, use a folding chair or countertop as your go-to surface. It doesn't matter where—it just matters that it helps you feel grounded. This is your staging space. Your off-ramp. A place where you can meet the clutter on your terms, one small batch at a time, in an environment that supports your brain instead of flooding it.

So when you feel your body saying, *This is too much*, it's not a reason to give up. It's an invitation to shift the scene. The Zen Zone helps you do just that.

Overwhelm Trigger: The Procrastination and Perfectionism Loop

Sometimes overwhelm doesn't only come from too much stuff—it comes from too much pressure to do it "the right way," the thorough way, the Pinterest-worthy way. That pressure often kicks off what I call the Procrastination and Perfectionism Loop.

It sounds like: *If I can't do it perfectly, I'll wait until I can*. So you wait—for the energy, the mood, the time, the perfect plan. But the longer we wait, the heavier it all feels. And that heavy feeling? It keeps us stuck.

There's research to back this up. A study in *Current Psychology* found that behavioral procrastination—delaying routine decisions and overdue tasks—was strongly linked to clutter across age groups. The same researchers showed that clutter was the best predictor of procrastination among adults.[4]

Why? Because clutter adds to the constant swirl of decisions, and when we feel that pressure to "do it all" or "do it perfectly," we freeze. We delay, then clutter builds again. It's a loop.

But here's what I want you to know when you find yourself there:

- You're not avoiding the task because you're lazy. You're avoiding the pressure of not doing it perfectly.
- You're not unmotivated. You're overwhelmed by the belief that progress only counts if it's big or complete.
- You're not behind. You're just believing a story that says small wins don't matter. (They do.)

So what's the way out?

Right-sized action. Not a giant leap or total room overhaul, just one small move—something light enough to get you moving, gentle enough to calm the pressure.

That's why we began this journey with resets. They're not just beginner tools; they're anchors you can return to again and again:

- You can clear the kitchen counter even if the pantry is still chaos.
- You can reset the living room without overhauling the toy bin.
- You can breathe easier after one drawer is cleared, even if the rest of the closet still needs work.

This movement regulates your nervous system. It breaks

the loop. It gives your brain and body a win it can actually process.

Take my student Caroline. She had been stuck for years waiting for the perfect weekend to tackle her hallway closet. Instead, she gave herself permission to start tiny: She tossed one expired medicine bottle during a clutter audit. That was it.

The next day, she let go of two more.

By the end of the week, she had cleared more than she thought possible, not because she finally had the right bins or the energy, but because she'd removed the pressure to do it all at once.

This is why I teach the 1 Percent Better Mindset.

Overwhelm Off-Ramp 2: The 1 Percent Better Mindset

This is a simple-yet-powerful approach popularized by James Clear in *Atomic Habits*. He shares how small, consistent improvements—just 1 percent better each day—can lead to remarkable change over time.[5]

In the decluttering world, that means interrupting perfectionism with tiny, doable actions. Instead of asking, *What should I be doing?* ask, *What's one small thing I can do today to make this space feel just 1 percent better?*

That's it. That's the exit.

It might be:

- tossing two empty shampoo bottles from the shower
- moving one donation into the car

- throwing away that appliance manual you've never opened

One small task is enough—because small is what sticks.

So the next time you feel that pressure creeping in, don't fight it with more effort. Meet it with less. Choose something light. Choose something now. And remind yourself: The goal isn't to be perfect. It's to keep going.

Keep Going, Your Way

Clutter Audits, 25 to Thrive, Zen Zones. They're not just methods—they're lifelines. Off-ramps. Anchors for the days that feel light and the ones that don't. They help you stay on the path when energy dips or life gets heavy. Let's stop chasing perfection. Let's build something we can return to.

My client Mia used to call herself "a chronic restarter." She'd try a new system every January, go all in for two weeks, and then burn out. Then she took a different approach: She gave herself permission to go slower. She started stacking small wins—one drawer, one clutter audit, one reset at a time.

Months later, she walked into her kitchen and caught herself smiling. "I didn't even realize I'd been following through," she told me. "But I am."

That's what we're after. Not more pressure, more trust. You don't need a perfect home to feel at home. You just need space to breathe, to belong, and to become. And you've already started. The point isn't how quickly you move; it's that you keep showing up—just like the tortoise. Step by steady step, you're doing the brave thing. You're still in the race.

REFLECT

When you look back on your progress so far, are there "small" moments that actually created big shifts?

Have you ever caught yourself in the Procrastination and Perfectionism Loop? What's the pressure you tend to put on yourself before you even start?

Which overwhelm off-ramp (Zen Zone or 1 Percent Better Mindset) feels most helpful to you right now?

TAKE ACTION

Try a Clutter Audit today in a space you already use—your bathroom, kitchen, or closet. Make one clear decision and move on.

Set a timer for twenty minutes this week and try a 25 to Thrive session in a spot that's been bothering you.

Create a Zen Zone—even if it's just a chair and a table. Use it as your calm place to make decisions when a space feels like too much.

Chapter 14

From Clutter to Clarity: The Life That's Waiting for You

If you take a long climb up a mountain and finally reach the top, there's a moment when your legs are burning, your lungs are catching up, and you finally turn around and take in the view. You realize you're not where you started. You have a different perspective.

The journey isn't over. You might still be carrying a load and have more peaks ahead. But now that you have a better sense of where you're headed and what you're capable of, you're starting to see everything differently.

Here, in the last chapter of this book, I hope you can see what matters and what you want. Maybe for the first time in a long time, you can picture a life that feels like yours again. At this point, I'm not giving you a checklist, a final exam, or even a claim that "you made it!" It's about what becomes possible now.

The space, the margin, the peace you've started to

Now that you have a better sense of where you're headed and what you're capable of, you're starting to see everything differently.

create? It's not just for the sake of tidy closets or clear counters. It's the launchpad to a life with more joy, more presence, more freedom. So let's stand here together for a second, look around, and talk about where you might want to go next.

Whether you've been actively decluttering or simply shifting your mindset as you've been reading this book, you aren't where you started. Early on, you might have been running on autopilot, like I once was. Managing. Fixing. Struggling to hold it all together while carrying the weight of clutter—physical, mental, and emotional.

But then you uncovered the hidden influences behind your clutter and challenged the old stories that made you feel stuck. You learned how to move beyond the surface and get to the roots of why clutter builds up, not only in your home but in your mind and heart too. You started to notice what adds value and what drains you, what you want to carry forward and what you're ready to let go of.

And now, here you are, viewing your home—and your life—through a new lens, maybe even seeing possibilities you hadn't been able to before. Standing at the edge of something new.

You're creating not only a simplified home but also a life where you have room to breathe, to dream, to be happier. Now it's time to envision yourself stepping fully into that space—with clarity and confidence, knowing that this is just the beginning.

The Power of Small Moments

Some of the most meaningful shifts don't show up on a checklist; they show up in the tiny, almost forgettable moments of your day.

Jenna used to stay up late most nights, wiping counters and folding laundry long after the rest of the house had gone quiet. She'd fall into bed exhausted and still feel like she was behind. But a few weeks into her new rhythm—one reset at a time, Clutter Audits here and there, a 25 to Thrive—something changed. It wasn't dramatic, but it was noticeable.

Her nightly cleanup, which used to take thirty minutes, slowly started taking less and less time because she was no longer battling so much clutter. That one shift, the gift of ten extra minutes, felt like reclaiming something she hadn't realized she'd lost. One night, she set the sponge down, lit a candle, and picked up a novel she hadn't opened in years. "I'd been waiting for a perfect moment to start reading again," she told me. "Turns out, I just needed a little breathing room."

That's the moment I want for you. And if it's not a novel, maybe it's sitting on the porch with your coffee. Maybe it's a walk around the block without your phone. Maybe it's whatever makes you feel most like yourself again.

These are the kinds of moments that signal something deeper has shifted—not only in your home, but in your spirit. They show up in subtle ways: when you exhale walking into your kitchen instead of bracing yourself. When wiping down the counters becomes a calming ritual instead of a chore. When you look around and realize, *My home isn't asking as much from me anymore.*

That kind of peace doesn't rush in; it builds. Quietly. Almost invisibly. At first, the strategies and systems will feel like work. But over time, they will become a rhythm. A muscle. A way of being. Resets that once took fifteen minutes now take five. The voice that always said *I'll get to it later* softens. And in the stillness, something beautiful begins. For some women, that stillness becomes space to heal.

After losing her mother, Carla couldn't bring herself to enter the guest room where they'd shared so many conversations. The room became a holding space for boxes, grief, and avoidance. But over time, she began to work through it—one drawer, one decision at a time. She didn't rush it. She just kept showing up.

Now it's a sun-filled space where she drinks tea and journals in the mornings. "It's where I go to feel close to her," she said. "It's where I let myself feel."

For others, space made way for creative momentum. Amanda, a graphic designer, always dreamed of painting for fun but felt too distracted in her own home. After decluttering her office nook and setting intentional limits on incoming items, she carved out a spot with just her paints, canvas, and music.

"It's nothing fancy," she told me, "but when I sit down to create, I feel like I'm remembering a version of myself I'd forgotten."

And sometimes, space leads to unexpected purpose. Jill, recently retired, used to say her home felt like a storage unit for her past careers and hobbies. After simplifying, she noticed she had the time and energy to do something she'd always put off: volunteering at a local literacy center. Now she spends one afternoon a week tutoring students, and she comes home energized.

"I thought I was just clearing space," she said. "Turns out, I was making room for purpose."

None of these women "finished" decluttering before they began living with more joy and intention. They didn't wait for the perfect room or the perfect moment. They simply started using their space, and their time, in ways that aligned with their values.

The truth is, the biggest transformation isn't found in a spotless closet. It's found in what becomes possible when your home stops getting in the way. When your space no longer drains you. Your capacity expands, bit by bit, so you're not simply surviving your days but stepping fully into them. Showing up with more presence, to create, to rest, or to reconnect with what makes you, you.

And then, often in the small moments, you'll find your home has started *giving back*: in peaceful mornings, in less friction, in more room to simply exist. As Anne Lamott once wrote, "Almost everything will work again if you unplug it for a few minutes—including you."[1]

This is what you're after. Not a perfect house or curated museum. But a home that works for you and supports a life that feels grounded and aligned.

The clutter you cleared? It was never the finish line. It was the doorway.

The clutter you cleared? It was never the finish line. It was the doorway.

To what?

More *emotional* space, *mental* space, *spiritual* space.

More freedom and possibility to build the life you want.

When Space Feels Uncomfortable

Here's the tricky thing about space: If we don't fill it with protective intention, the noise will rush back in.

For so many of us, being busy isn't just a habit. It's an identity. We measure the success of a day by how much we accomplished. We equate *rest* with *laziness*. And when we finally do find a sliver of time, our first instinct is to fill it with another task, another errand, another to-do. At first, the open space can feel unnatural. You sit down and feel the urge to get back up. You have ten free minutes and instinctively look for something to clean. Stillness feels lazy. Rest feels like you're doing something wrong.

But that discomfort? It's not a sign you're failing. It's a sign you're deprogramming. You're learning how to exist outside the hamster wheel. You're learning how to belong to yourself again, not just to your to-do list.

Maybe you haven't had those moments yet, or they've been few and far between. After years of reacting to clutter and pressure, your nervous system might still crave motion. You might feel the itch to fix, to manage, to keep moving—even when the constant, urgent demands have lifted. That blank space on your calendar, or your countertop, might feel unsettling at first. But it's not emptiness; it's possibility.

Slow down. Look around. See that stillness isn't laziness; it's healing.

This margin—the one you're working diligently to create—isn't empty. It's sacred.

The Space Between Where You Were and What Comes Next

Most women haven't made space for themselves in years, so when they encounter open spaces full of possibility, they find themselves at a loss. New questions surface. *Where has my time and energy been going? Where do I want it to go?*

Remember the vision you set out for yourself when you described *why* you wanted to simplify—when you named your *Big Why*. Think back to that now as you envision how you want to use your sacred new space. And consider what some of my clients have done with theirs.

Stephanie cleared out her craft room, a space that had

been packed with half-finished projects and bins labeled "someday," then she turned it into a cozy writing nook. It became her spot to go sit with a cup of tea and open her journal. Just a few minutes a day turned into something bigger—a quiet ritual that helped her reconnect with a version of herself she thought was long gone. Now she says, "This little corner of the house feels like mine. It feels like home."

Brianna used to spend every Saturday tackling the house from top to bottom. She'd clean bathrooms, vacuum, do laundry, and tidy up every room while her husband took the kids out. It became her routine, but it left her exhausted, resentful, and disconnected from the family time she had wanted all along.

As she began decluttering, she noticed that her home didn't take as long to clean anymore. She no longer needed a marathon session every weekend to keep things running smoothly. So she shifted to deeper cleaning once a month and handled smaller resets during the week. That one change gave her Saturdays back.

Now, she and her family go for nature walks on Saturdays. Her youngest always brings back a rock or a flower. "There are still messes sometimes," she says, "but my time is finally going where I want it to."

Nicole reclaimed her mornings. Instead of rushing into the day and feeling distracted by a stressful space, she lights a candle, pours a cup of coffee, and reads her Bible. Just ten minutes of quiet anchors her. "It reminds me who I am before the day starts telling me who to be," she said. It's simple, sacred, and entirely hers.

Did these women "finish" decluttering before they

started doing these things? No. But they made enough space. And that space helped them come home—not only to a tidy room, but to themselves.

That was part of their Big Why.

What about you? What will you choose to do with this space?

Start imagining it now.

You might be more present with your family and friends—not just physically there, but emotionally available. Laughing without your mind wandering to laundry. Lingering over conversations without mentally reciting tomorrow's to-do list.

You might sit in your kitchen with nothing to do and feel at peace. Or blast music and have a spontaneous dance party while you fold towels. You might dust off the parts of yourself buried under years of "someday." The creative spark or spontaneous idea. The hobby you once loved. The dream you tucked away years ago. You might host a game night, start a garden, roll out a yoga mat, paint with your kids, pick wildflowers, join a local rec team, or have a slow breakfast on a Tuesday just because you can. Not because it's productive. Not because anyone will see it. But because you matter.

You can rediscover joy—not in completing a checklist but in feeling light. In catching your reflection and seeing someone at ease. In belonging to your life again.

That version of you—the joyful, present, whole version—has always been there. She's just been waiting for space to reemerge.

So here's what I want you to do: Go sit in a space you've cleared.

Don't clean. Don't scroll. Don't fix. Just be.

Let yourself breathe in the lightness. Let yourself feel what it's like to live in a home that no longer demands so much from you.

When Life Gets Messy, You'll Be Okay

Life isn't a fairy tale, and your clutter doesn't come with a fairy godmother. So let's be honest—things will get messy again. The dog will shed. The laundry will rebel. Someone will get sick. The junk drawer will once again live up to its name. Your kitchen counter, once clear, might become a drop zone again. And that little voice might whisper, *Here we go again*.

But these are the kinds of moments you've been preparing for. The feel-good seasons of simplicity are built to carry you through the hard ones. This time, you'll respond differently because you are different. You no longer see your home, or your life, the same way.

You know how to reset and how to tune in instead of spiral. You have a deeper understanding of what your space is telling you and what you need. You've practiced letting go of what's no longer serving you and choosing the kind of life you want to live. You have systems and rhythms to return to.

The more you act like a simplifier, the more you'll become one. Day after day, you'll be someone who is no longer managing chaos but instead creating calm. Every reset, every Clutter Audit, every 25 to Thrive session—each one will be a declaration of who you are becoming. This isn't just about keeping your house tidy. This is about becoming someone who can find her way back to clarity, over and over again.

When life feels loud, you can come back to yourself. When you hit a messy moment, pause and ask: *What was I doing when life felt lighter? What tiny rhythm made me feel steady? What's one small thing I can do right now to move forward?* Maybe it's a quick reset before bed. Or a Clutter Audit in your car. Maybe it's turning on a favorite playlist and doing a five-minute reset with your family, laughing as you go. It doesn't have to be big. It just has to be forward.

Remember that clutter is a signal, not a setback. A gentle tap on the shoulder, not a judgment. And you're not starting over. You're simply continuing.

The climb isn't over, but your view is clearer and you know exactly how to keep going. One small step at a time. Progress might feel slow, but slow progress is still progress. You're not behind; you're becoming.

I hope there are times you walk into your space and, whether it's freshly reset or just real-life messy, something inside you says, *This is mine. I built this peace, one drawer, one decision, one imperfect day at a time.* That's not just progress; that's power. Even if you drift from your rhythms, you know how to return. You know what matters, what adds value, and what you're no longer willing to carry.

This book isn't a checklist; it's a companion. Come back to it anytime you need a nudge, a reset, or a reminder that progress doesn't have to be fast or flawless to be real. You don't need a perfect home to feel at home. You just need space to breathe, to belong, and to become. And you've already started.

Notes

Chapter 2

1. Bruce H. Lipton, "Is There a Way to Change Subconscious Patterns?," March 10, 2025, https://www.brucelipton.com/there-way-change-subconscious-patterns/.
2. Jennifer Fisher, "Tips to Leverage Neuroplasticity to Maintain Cognitive Fitness as You Age," Harvard Health Publishing, April 2, 2025, https://www.health.harvard.edu/mind-and-mood/tips-to-leverage-neuroplasticity-to-maintain-cognitive-fitness-as-you-age.

Chapter 3

1. Donald W. Winnicott, *The Maturational Processes and the Facilitating Environment: Studies in the Theory of Emotional Development* (Routledge, 2018), 109.
2. Brené Brown, *Daring Greatly* (Gotham Books, 2012), 189.
3. June P. Tangney, Jeffrey Stuewig, and Andres G. Martinez, "Two Faces of Shame: The Roles of Shame and Guilt in Predicting Recidivism," *Psychological Science* 25, no. 3 (2014): 799–805, DOI: 10.1177/0956797613508790.

Chapter 4

1. The Minimalists, "Getting Rid of Just-in-Case Items: 20 Dollars, 20 Minutes," The Minimalists, accessed July 14, 2025, https://www.theminimalists.com/jic/.

Chapter 5

1. Susi Hately, host, *From Pain to Possibility* podcast, episode #212, "Feeling Your Body and Losing Weight with Corinne Crabtree," November 23, 2023, https://functionalsynergy.com/feeling-your-body-and-losing-weight-with-corinne-crabtree-ep-212/; full episode transcript: https://www.functionalsynergy.com/wp-content/uploads/2024/07/FPTP-Transcript-212.pdf.
2. David E. Bell, "Regret in Decision Making Under Uncertainty," *Operations Research* 30, no. 5 (1982): 961–81, https://www.jstor.org/stable/170353; Graham Loomes and Robert Sugden, "Regret Theory: An Alternative Theory of Rational Choice Under Uncertainty," *Economic Journal* 92, no. 368 (1982): 805–24, https://doi.org/10.2307/2232669.

Chapter 6

1. Karen Page Winterich, Rebecca W. Reczek, and Julie R. Irwin, "Keeping the Memory but Not the Possession: Memory Preservation Mitigates Identity Loss from Product Disposition," *Journal of Marketing* 81, no. 5 (2017): 105–23, DOI:10.1509/jm.16.0311.

Chapter 7

1. Daniel Kahneman, *Thinking, Fast and Slow* (Farrar, Straus and Giroux, 2011), 292–93.

Chapter 8

1. Darby E. Saxbe and Rena L. Repetti, "No Place Like Home: Home Tours Correlate with Daily Patterns of Mood and Cortisol," *Personality and Social Psychology Bulletin* 36, no. 1 (2010): 71–81, doi: 10.1177/0146167209352864.
2. Joshua Becker, "20 Quotes That Will Change the Way You See Your Stuff," Becoming Minimalist, September 22, 2020, www.becomingminimalist.com/20-quotes-that-will-change-the-way-you-see-your-stuff.

Chapter 9

1. James Clear, *Atomic Habits: An Easy & Proven Way to Build Good Habits and Break Bad Ones* (Avery, 2018), 27.

Chapter 10

1. Clear, *Atomic Habits*, 70.
2. Joseph R. Ferrari and Catherine A. Roster, "Delaying Disposing: Examining the Relationship between Procrastination and Clutter across Generations," *Current Psychology* 37, no. 2 (2018): 426–31, https://link.springer.com/article/10.1007/s12144-017-9679-4.

Chapter 11

1. Eve Rodsky, *Fair Play: A Game-Changing Solution for When You Have Too Much to Do (and More Life to Live)* (G.P. Putnam's Sons, 2019), 15.
2. Becky Kennedy, *Good Inside with Dr. Becky*, podcast, "Connect to the Good Kid Underneath the Bad Behavior," February 4, 2025, https://podscripts.co/podcasts/good-inside-with-dr-becky/connect-to-the-good-kid-underneath-the-bad-behavior.
3. David Wood, Jerome S. Bruner, and Gail Ross, "The Role of Tutoring in Problem Solving," *Journal of Child Psychology and Psychiatry* 17, no 2: (2006), 89–100, DOI:10.1111/j.1469-7610.1976.tb00381.x.
4. Becky Kennedy, "How to Get Kids to Listen Without Yelling or Power Struggles," *Good Inside*, accessed October 20, 2025, https://www.goodinside.com/blog/how-to-get-kids-to-listen/.
5. Grace Koelma, *The ADHD Focus Friend: A Planning & Productivity Workbook* (Penguin, 2025), 111.
6. Thomas E. Brown, *Smart but Stuck: Emotions in Teens and Adults with ADHD* (Jossey-Bass, 2014), 2.
7. Brown, *Smart but Stuck*, 17.

Chapter 12

1. Andrew Huberman, "Controlling Your Dopamine for Motivation, Focus and Satisfaction," *Huberman Lab*, podcast, episode 39, YouTube, September 27, 2021, https://www.youtube.com/watch?v=QmOF0crdyRU.
2. Kent C. Berridge and Terry E. Robinson, "Parsing Reward," *Trends in Neurosciences* 26, no. 9 (2003): 507–13, https://doi.org/10.1016/S0166-2236(03)00233-9.

Chapter 13

1. David I. Donaldson, Mark E. Wheeler, and Steve E. Petersen, "Remember the Source: Dissociating Frontal and Parietal Contributions to Episodic Memory," *Journal of Cognitive Neuroscience* 22, no. 2 (2010): 377–91, as referenced in Philippe Hong, "Pomodoro Myths and Does It Actually Work?" Founder Foundry, January 17, 2025, https://www.founderfoundry.com/article/pomodoro-myths-and-does-it-actually-work.
2. Amanda Reill, "A Simple Way to Make Better Decisions," *Harvard Business Review*, December 5, 2023, https://hbr.org/2023/12/a-simple-way-to-make-better-decisions.
3. Jeanne E. Arnold, Anthony P. Graesch, Enzo Ragazzini, and Elinor Ochs, *Life at Home in the Twenty-First Century: 32 Families Open Their Doors* (Cotsen Institute of Archaeology Press, 2012); see also Erika Penney, "Why Household Mess Triggers Stress and Anxiety," *Neuroscience News*, September 4, 2023, https://neurosciencenews.com/anxiety-stress-messy-home-23874/.
4. Joseph R. Ferrari and Catherine A. Roster, "Delaying Disposing: Examining the Relationship between Procrastination and Clutter across Generations," *Current Psychology* 37, no. 2 (2018): 426–31, https://link.springer.com/article/10.1007/s12144-017-9679-4.
5. Clear, *Atomic Habits*, 13.

Chapter 14

1. Anne Lamott, *Small Victories: Spotting Improbable Moments of Grace* (Riverhead Books, 2014), 43.

About the Author

Katy Joy Wells is a former overwhelmed mom turned top decluttering expert and the host of the widely loved podcast *The Maximized Minimalist,* listened to over five million times. Through her bestselling programs and podcast, Katy has helped hundreds of thousands of women and families break free from clutter, lighten their mental load, and finally feel like themselves again.

Known for her holistic approach to decluttering, Katy helps women go beyond surface-level strategies by addressing the emotional and psychological roots of clutter—so they can shift their habits, mindsets, and homes in ways that actually last.

She's a repeat guest on *NBC News Daily* and has been featured in *Real Simple, Martha Stewart Living, Better Homes & Gardens,* and more. Katy lives in Asheville, North Carolina, with her husband, Andrew, and their two boys. Learn more at KatyJoyWells.com.